HISTORIC AMERICAN BUILDINGS

SURVEY IN INDIANA

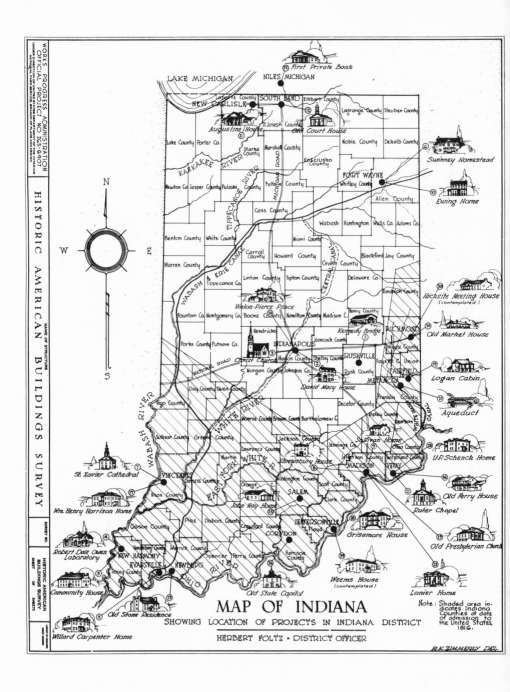

N
W E
S

First Private Bank

LAKE MICHIGAN
NILES MICHIGAN

NEW CARLISLE
SOUTH BEND
Elkhart County
Laporte County
St. Joseph County
Old Court House
Lagrange County
Steuben County

Augustine House
Lake County Porter Co.
Starke County
Marshall County
Noble County
DeKalb County

Swinney Homestead

KANKAKEE RIVER
Kosciusko County
FORT WAYNE
Whitley County
Allen County

Ewing Home

Newton Co Jasper County Pulaski County
Fulton County
Michigan Road

Cass County
Wabash Huntington Wells Co. Adams Co.

Benton County White County
Carroll County
Howard County
Miami County
Blackford Jay County

Warren County
Grant County

WABASH & ERIE CANAL
Tippecanoe Co.
Linton County
Tipton County
Delaware Co.
Randolph County

Hicksite Meeting House (contemplated)

Vinton-Pierce Place
Fountain Co. Montgomery Co. Boone County
Hamilton County Madison Co.
Henry County
Kennedy Bridge
RICHMOND
Old Market House

Hendricks
Parke County Putnam Co.
INDIANAPOLIS
Hancock County
Wayne County
Fayette & Union
FAIRFIELD

Logan Cabin

NATIONAL ROAD
CHRIST CHURCH
Marion County
Shelby County
RUSHVILLE
Rush County
METAMORA

Clay County Owen County
Morgan County Johnson Co.
David Macy House
Franklin County

WABASH RIVER
Vigo County
WHITE RIVER
Decatur County
Ripley County
Aqueduct

St. Xavier Cathedral
Sullivan County Greene County
Monroe County Brown County Bartholomew C.
Sullivan Home
Ohio Co.
U.P. Schenck Home

VINCENNES
E. FORK WHITE R.
Jackson County
Jennings Co.
MADISON
VEVAY

Wm. Henry Harrison Home
Knox County
Martin
Lawrence County
WHITE R.
Shrewsbury House
Jefferson County Switzerland County
Old Ferry House

Robert Dale Owen Laboratory
Daviess County
Orange C.
Washington County
Scott County
Ruter Chapel

Community House
Gibson County
John Hay Home
SALEM
Clark County
Old Presbyterian Church

NEW HARMONY
EVANSVILLE
NEWBURG
Pike Dubois County
Crawford County
JEFFERSONVILLE
Floyd
Grisamore House

Vanderburg County
Warrick County
Spencer Perry County
CORYDON
Harrison County
Weems House (contemplated)

Lanier Home

Posey County
OHIO RIVER
Old State Capitol

Old Stone Residences

Willard Carpenter Home

MAP OF INDIANA
SHOWING LOCATION OF PROJECTS IN INDIANA DISTRICT
HERBERT FOLTZ · DISTRICT OFFICER

Note: Shaded area indicates Indiana Counties at date of admission to the United States 1816.

R.K. ZIMMERLY DEL.

HISTORIC AMERICAN BUILDINGS SURVEY IN

INDIANA

EDITED BY

Thomas M. Slade

Published for Historic Landmarks Foundation

of Indiana • Indianapolis

by Indiana University Press • Bloomington

Manufactured in the United States of America

Library of Congress Cataloging in Publication Data

Main entry under title:

Historic American Buildings Survey in Indiana.

    Includes index.
    1. Historical buildings—Indiana. 2. Historic American Buildings
Survey. I. Slade, Thomas M., 1942–
NA730.I6H57   1983   720'.9772   83–47992
ISBN 0–253–32741–5
ISBN 0–253–21295–2 (pbk.)
1 2 3 4 5 87 86 85 84 83

Contents

Foreword

By the time Historic Landmarks Foundation of Indiana (HLFI) was organized in 1960, the Historic American Buildings Survey (HABS)—with support from the Indiana Chapter of the American Institute of Architects—had already recorded nearly fifty structures throughout the state. The HABS program of measuring, drawing, and photographing historic buildings set a high standard for the documentation of Indiana's significant historic architecture that the fledgling HLFI—a private membership organization—incorporated into the wording of its founding charter.

For the past twenty-three years, HLFI has coordinated, funded, and otherwise assisted in the HABS program, and this catalog therefore represents nearly a quarter-century of partnership between HABS and HLFI. A wide variety of structural types, from factory buildings to grand mansions, are depicted in the catalog's 161 entries, illustrated with 33 photographs and 51 line drawings. Of the 161 documented buildings, 23 have been destroyed and 7 have been moved from their original sites. The catalog also contains entries for 12 historic districts comprising a total of 64 buildings.

It is appropriate to note that HABS recording activities have led to other significant documentation programs in Indiana. Chief among these is the curriculum of Ball State University's College of Architecture and Planning, which stresses the importance of measured drawings and accurate recording procedures. Since 1966, Ball State has contributed over 430 original measured drawings to the HABS archives maintained by the Library of Congress in Washington, D.C.

Another long-term supporter of HABS in Indiana, the Indiana Historical Society, has established architectural archives in response to local demand. Under the auspices of the society's library, the Committee for the Preservation of Architectural Records oversees the acquisition and preservation of collections from many of Indiana's most noted architects, designers, and engineers.

Through the Division of Historic Preservation and Archaeology of the Department of Natural Resources, the State of Indiana has also contributed to the documentation of Indiana's historic architecture by developing a methodology for documenting threatened buildings and those structures deemed singularly significant as cultural resources. In addition, that office has issued a statewide preservation plan that calls for the inventory of historic sites and structures in compliance with the National Historic Preservation Act of 1966. Since 1973, HLFI has been the major contractor for this comprehensive survey project. Inventories of twenty-seven of Indiana's ninety-two counties have been completed.

This catalog is the result of the work of many individuals and has depended on the cooperation of many organizations. It is published as a testament to the richness of Indiana's historic architecture and as a reference for scholars, preservationists, and those who simply enjoy and appreciate old buildings. The year of publication appropriately falls on the fiftieth anniversary of the founding of HABS, a program that continues to expand our awareness of the value of Indiana's architectural history.

J. REID WILLIAMSON, JR.
President
Historic Landmarks Foundation of Indiana

Acknowledgments

The editor is greatly indebted to numerous individuals and organizations who have waited patiently for the completion of this catalog of the Historic American Buildings Survey efforts in Indiana. Unfortunately, it is not possible to mention the names of all those who provided information for specific sites, have served as stewards and saviors of Indiana's architectural resources, or have worked on the publication of this catalog.

I should, however, like to make special mention of those at the Historic American Buildings Survey who have assisted this project over the years: J. Allen Chambers and Nancy Schwartz, architectural historians; Alicia Stamm, archivist; Robert Kapsch, chief; James C. Massey and John C. Poppeliers, the former directors who negotiated the revival of recording activities in the 1950s, 1960s, and 1970s; and especially Jack Boucher, who drove the roads of Indiana to photograph the sites. At the Library of Congress, Mary Ison and Ford Petross have been especially helpful in cataloging and maintaining the records.

It is also important to acknowledge the early assistance of the Indiana Historical Society. Hubert H. Hawkins, former director, served on the committee that selected the sites in the 1950s, and Gayle Thornbrough, the present director, helped arrange cooperative funding for the work accomplished in the 1970s.

Information regarding many sites was provided by the following individuals: Barbara Abel, Conner Prairie Pioneer Settlement; William Ahrendt, Augsburg Swensk Skola; Mr. and Mrs. D. I. Alcorn, Lantz House; Delores Baker, "Hillforest"; Geraldine Baldwin, Benton House; C. A. Bonsett, Pathological Department Building; Jon Bonstrator, Earlham College Observatory; Rita Boone, McNaughton House; Dick Brandt, Ridgeville Switching Station; C. Claric Brown, Bailly House; Mrs. Herbert Brown, Stout House; Mr.

and Mrs. R. G. Coplin, Fussell Log House; Mrs. Ben Daniels, Daniels House; Mr. and Mrs. Mark Helt, Wright House; Herbert Hill, Daniel Copple House; Opal Hines, Devenish-Haigh House; Lee Hougland, Gray House; Fran Julian, "Tudor Hall"; Richard Kline, Washington Fire Company No. 2; Kendra Lininger, Bruning Carriage House; Kenneth O. Hannum and Dr. and Mrs. John Logan, Dewees House; Mr. and Mrs. Robert McGuire, Coffin House; Pauline Montgomery, Conklin House; Maurice Paton, Ames-Paton House; E. L. Ringenburg, Adams House; Mr. and Mrs. Hisle Rippey, Robinson-Schofield House; Mr. and Mrs. Richard Sommers, "Tudor Hall"; Mr. and Mrs. John Windle, Shrewsbury House; Evans Woollen, Indiana Theater; Nancy Long, Division of Historic Preservation and Archaeology, Department of Natural Resources.

In addition, the compilers' and the editor's efforts were greatly facilitated by the cooperation of Mrs. Edward Van Riper, Philip and Peter Roberson, Karen Niggle, James Long, Rebecca Reiff, and Christine Connor.

Historic Landmarks Foundation of Indiana wishes to pay special tribute to Edward James, FAIA, who saw the need to record and preserve the architectural heritage of Indiana. Without his interest, concern, and dedication, many of the buildings lost would never have been documented and many others that stand today would have not been identified and rescued from neglect.

List of Abbreviations

The following abbreviations have been used in all recent HABS catalogs.

(IN-56)   INDIANA-56. Historic American Buildings Survey number. All structures recorded by the survey are assigned a final Indiana number by the HABS Washington office. These numbers ought to be used in ordering reproductions of HABS materials.

sheets   Sheets of measured architectural drawings recorded for each entry. The date(s) and kinds of drawings (plans, sections, elevations, and so on) are indicated in parentheses.

photos   Photographs. Exterior and/or interior. Unless otherwise noted, all HABS photographs are black and white. HABS negatives are normally 5 × 7 inches, but are sometimes other sizes, especially 4 × 5 inches and 8 × 10 inches.

photocopy   Photographic copy or reproduction. Photocopies include photographic facsimilies of old maps, sketches, drawings, photographs, and other historical material pertaining to each recorded structure.

data pages   Data pages of architectural and historical information recorded about each building. Original data pages are typewritten on one side of the page only.

n.d.	No date. The exact date or dates are not ascertainable at present.
ext./int.	Exterior/interior.
HABSI form	Historic American Buildings Survey Inventory form. A one-page, front-and-back information form on file in the HABS archives in the Library of Congress. Each form contains identification of the structure, concise written architectural and/or historical data, a small photograph, a location diagram, and source references on an 8 × 10½ inch format. See Appendix A of this catalog for a complete list of HABSI structures in Indiana.
HAER	Historic American Engineering Record. Indicates that a HABS building has also been recorded by the Historic American Engineering Record as significant in the history of American engineering and technology. See Appendix B of this catalog for a complete listing of HAER structures in Indiana.
NHL	National Historic Landmark. Indicates that a HABS structure has been declared a National Historic Landmark by the secretary of the interior. National Historic Landmarks are listed automatically on the National Register of Historic Places, but are also given NR designation in this catalog.
NR	National Register of Historic Places. Indicates that a HABS structure has been placed on the National Register of Historic Places by the secretary of the interior. If the structure is located within a historic district, but not specifically listed on the National Register, the name of the historic district follows in parentheses.

Historic American Buildings Survey: An Introduction

The Historic American Buildings Survey (HABS) is an ongoing program to assemble national archives of historic American architecture. Begun in November 1933 as a Civil Works Administration (CWA) project to provide necessary funds for unemployed architects and draftsmen, the survey represented one of the federal government's first major steps toward the identification and preservation of historic structures. The CWA project, which officially terminated in May 1934, proved so successful that on July 23, 1934, a Memorandum of Agreement was drafted by the National Park Service, the American Institute of Architects, and the Library of Congress recognizing HABS as a permanent organization responsible for coordinating all future recording of historic American buildings. This tripartite agreement has served, for the most part, as the operating basis of the HABS program. HABS administers the survey and is responsible for the establishment of qualitative standards, the organization of field projects, and the selection of sites and structures to be recorded. The Library of Congress acts as the depository for the architectural data serviced by its Division of Prints and Photographs. The American Institute of Architects provides professional counsel through its national organization and regional offices.

The active recording program of HABS was terminated at the outbreak of World War II, but recognition of the continuing value of the program led to its reactivation in 1957, and extensive recording has gone on since then. In 1967, HABS, along with other historic preservation programs of the National Park Service, was placed in the Office of Archaeology and Historic Preservation (OAHP), supervised by the chief of the survey. On January 25, 1978, by Order No. 3017 of the U.S. secretary of the interior, OAHP was combined with the Department of the Interior's Bureau of Outdoor Recreation and its Natural Landmarks Program to form the Heritage Conservation and Recreation Service (HCRS) as a new agency of the Department of the Interior. Administrative responsibility for both HABS and the Historic American Engineering Record (HAER, created in 1969) was given to the office of the National Architectural and Engineering Record (NAER). In 1981, HCRS was abolished, and the HABS program was returned to the National Park Service. Both HABS and HAER are currently (1983) administered under NAER.

The goal of HABS has been to develop the broadest possible coverage for all themes, periods, styles, and types of American architecture. Sites and structures represented in the survey span the period from prehistoric and colonial times to the late nineteenth and early twentieth centuries, and include examples from all fifty states, the District of Columbia, Puerto Rico, and the Virgin Islands. Since 1933, thousands of records comprising architectural measured drawings, photographs, and data sheets have been collected and deposited in HABS' permanent archive in the Library of Congress. The collection now includes more than 16,000 buildings represented by over 31,000 drawings, 47,000 photographs, and 23,500 pages of written data sheets.

Those who are interested in consulting HABS records may either visit the Division of Prints and Photographs in the Library of Congress or consult the published HABS catalogs. A comprehensive, geographically arranged *Catalog* was published in 1941 (reprint, 1971); an updated *Supplement* appeared in 1959. More recently, because of the extensiveness of HABS documentation, separate catalogs are being published by individual states and local metropolitan areas. To date, state catalogs have appeared for New Hampshire (1963), Massachusetts (1965, 1976), Wisconsin (1965), Michigan (1967), Utah (1969), Maine (1974), Texas (1974), Virginia (1975), New Jersey (1977), and Iowa (1979). Catalogs for Chicago and nearby Illinois areas (1966), the District of Columbia (1974), and Philadelphia (1976) have also been published. Most of these publications can be consulted in major university or public libraries.

Questions regarding the consultation of HABS records or the ordering of reproductions may be addressed to

> Division of Prints and Photographs
> Library of Congress
> Washington, D.C. 20540

Questions regarding the HABS recording and publishing program should be addressed to

> Historic American Buildings Survey
> National Park Service
> Department of the Interior
> Washington, D.C. 20243

In 1970, the National Park Service published *Recording Historic Buildings*, compiled by Harley J. McKee. Based on the survey's long experience and now widely regarded as the definitive work in the field, this volume has established standards and procedures for gathering both historical and architectural documentation. Copies may be purchased from

> Superintendent of Documents
> U.S. Government Printing Office
> Washington, D.C. 20402

About the HABS Indiana Catalog

This publication is the catalog of all 161 entries for Indiana recorded by the Historic American Buildings Survey (HABS) from 1934 through December 1979. It contains expanded and updated listings from the 1941 and 1959 national catalogs as well as new entries for additional structures recorded from 1959 through 1979. Initial field data was checked in the summer of 1970 by architectural historian William P. Thompson. All entries surveyed before 1970 and those structures recorded in 1970, 1971, and 1974 were edited, updated, and enlarged by Nancy B. Schwartz of the Washington HABS office. In September 1980, after still further editorial work, Historic Landmarks Foundation of Indiana contracted with Samuel A. Roberson, Associate Professor of Architectural History, Indiana University-Indianapolis, and Sheryl D. Roberson, historian and genealogist, to prepare a completely updated typescript catalog. All entries were carefully checked in the field for accuracy of information and description. Forty-one new entries (IN-121 through IN-161) were written for structures recorded by the survey since 1974, principally those entries from 1978, the year of the last intensive Indiana HABS field activity.

Each HABS catalog entry contains a concise description and historical account, and lists the type and quantity of HABS records compiled for each documented structure. The entries are organized geographically by town or city, followed by its county location and, in parentheses, its county code number. Entries not located within a town or city limits are listed as being in the vicinity of its nearest town or city—Madison Vicinity, Waterloo Vicinity, for example. Locations and addresses have been listed as accurately as possible so that this catalog can serve as a field guide for visiting the structures listed. The catalog format for the entries follows this order: historic name, when known; HABS Indiana number; address; brief physical description, including construction materials, dimensions, number of stories, roof type, and important exterior and interior details; date(s) of construction; architect and builder, if known; alterations and additions; academic style; important historical facts; and a listing of the measured drawings, photographs, photocopies, and data pages available in the HABS archives in the Library of Congress. Many of the buildings recorded by HABS have been recognized as National Historic Landmarks (NHL) or either as individual buildings on the National Register of Historic Places (NR) or as part of a National Register historic district; these designations are indicated in the catalog as NHL and NR, with a historic district in parentheses, following the complete entry.

Appended to the catalog are listings of the Historic American Buildings Survey Inventory (HABSI) and the Historic American Engineering Record (HAER) for Indiana. Appendix A contains a complete listing of the 76 HABSI forms. The HABSI recording program was initiated in 1953 jointly by the American Institute of Architects, the National Trust for Historic Preservation, and the National Park Service to provide basic field information on buildings throughout the United States, Puerto Rico, and the Virgin Islands. When HABS was reactivated in 1957, the inventory recording program became subordinate to the more comprehensive survey. The one-page, two-side inventory form was designed to be filled out in the field by interested individuals and concerned preservation groups. The need for inventory forms declined with the expansion of the National Register after the National Historic Preservation Act of 1966, and the form was finally discontinued in 1970. The HABSI forms on file in the Library of Congress constitute, however, an important companion collection to the HABS records.

Appendix B contains entries for all 46 HAER structures recorded in Indiana between 1969 and 1981. Each entry description was expanded from the 1976 *Historic American Engineering Record Catalog* compiled by Donald E. Sackheim. The descriptive information sequence was changed to conform to the HABS catalog format.

It should be understood that this catalog is not a definitive listing of all worthwhile historic architecture is Indiana but is, rather, a comprehensive record of the HABS materials transmitted to the Library of Congress archives through December 1979. Numerous important buildings remain to be recorded. New entries will be added as HABS recording in Indiana continues.

HISTORIC AMERICAN BUILDINGS
SURVEY IN INDIANA

HABS in Indiana, 1933–1940

David R. Hermansen

The Civil Works Administration (CWA) organized and commenced in December 1933 a program to document important examples of America's architectural legacy, as well as to provide "A Ten Week Unemployment Relief Project for One Thousand Architects and Architectural Draftsmen." Indiana was designated district number 24. Herbert W. Foltz, a well-known Indianapolis architect and past president of the local chapter of the American Institute of Architects (AIA), was selected to be the district officer. The district was allotted twenty-eight participants.[1]

The first twenty buildings selected were distributed throughout the populated areas of the state. All the structures except the first, the Kennedy Covered Bridge (IN-1), were built before 1860. The oldest building recorded, "Grouseland" (IN-17) in Vincennes, now operated as a house museum by the Daughters of the American Revolution, was built in 1803–04 for William Henry Harrison, governor of the Northwest Territory. The house was both his home and military headquarters, with the west parlor used as the council chamber. Constructed by William Lindsey, Grouseland is the most impressive early example of the Federal architecture in the state. "Its plan is said to be similar to the plan of Berkeley, on the James River in Virginia, Harrison's birth place."[2] The rectangular two-and-a-half-story main brick block has a curved projecting bay on the west elevation. The house is elevated on a high base and, with a high hipped roof, recalls similar Georgian examples in Virginia. Modest but classically detailed, one-story porches shelter the south and east entrances. Timber was cut at the site, brick was locally burned, but window glass came from Boston and the mantels from London. The architect of Grouseland is uncertain, but it is more than likely that Harrison himself designed this well-proportioned and handsomely detailed residence.

1

Other Federal-style houses surveyed in the initial work period included the Jeremiah Sullivan House (IN-9) in Madison, the Grisamore House (IN-18) in Jeffersonville, and the Gaines Hardy Roberts House (IN-13) at Newburgh, overlooking the Ohio River. The Sullivan House, built in 1818, is an L-shaped two-story block on a very tall base. The most notable feature of the house is the finely proportioned and detailed main entrance with elliptical fanlights and narrow sidelights flanked by attenuated colonnettes, outlined with beading. Less than a block away is the Robinson-Schofield House (IN-82), built about the same time as the Sullivan House and similar to it in plan and form.

The Gaines Hardy Roberts House (IN-13), built c. 1835, is a finely proportioned stone two-story building. It has massive, projecting paired end chimneys of rubble stone connected by parapets similar to those of the Sullivan House. Paired end chimneys became a trademark during this period in Indiana. The five-bay facade is of dressed stone, as are the window surrounds. The windows are deeply recessed. The central entry, defined by an arched opening, has double doors and a semicircular fanlight. The kitchen extension was added in 1931 and a two-story classically inspired projecting porch was added after 1935 to protect the entry and balcony.

Midway along the Ohio River between the cities of Madison and Newburgh is Jeffersonville, where stands the Grisamore House, built 1837–38 (IN-18). The Grisamore House appears to be a single structure of typical Federal-style proportion and details as in its fenestration and paired end chimneys. However, the classical temple pediment capping the three engaged Tuscan doric columns hides the paired entrances to what is actually a double residence. The relationship between the two units is very unusual in the alternations between straight and curved lines as seen in the portico lintel and the balcony railings. In 1981, a fire in the west unit of the house completely gutted the living quarters west of the stair hall and destroyed the roof. Local preservationists have completely rehabilitated and restored the building for use as commercial office space. The project was greatly facilitated by the existence of HABS drawings and photographs made in 1934. Historic Landmarks Foundation of Indiana assisted in the restoration and has located its southern regional office there.

Recognizing the importance of religious architecture, and the people and history it represented, the initial project included three religious structures ranging in date of construction from 1826 to 1857. The three buildings are also of three different styles. On March 30, 1826, on the site of the late-eighteenth-century French chapel in Vincennes, the cornerstone of Saint Francis Xavier Cathedral was laid. The building was enclosed in 1834, but it was not until 1850 that the interior appointments, tower, and spire were completed. The plan and interior of Saint Francis Xavier are similar to those of Saint Joseph's Church (formerly Cathedral) in Bardstown, Kentucky, built between 1816 and 1819. Vincennes was in the jurisdiction of the Bardstown diocese, led by Bishop Flaget. Earlier in his career, Bishop Flaget had been assigned to Vincennes, and it is quite probable that he encouraged the Reverend J. B. Champomier to base the design of Saint Francis Xavier on the excellent Kentucky precedent, Saint Joseph's. Although the facade of Saint Francis Xavier was built during the Classical Revival period, it is more indicative of the late Georgian and Federal styles. The simple brick pedimented facade has three widely spaced semicircular arched doorways with similarly arched niches above for sculpture. The tympanum is pierced by a well-scaled bull's eye. The tower, with its spire capped with a cross, rises 102 feet above the apex of the pediment. Except for the low brick base, the tower and spire are of timber sheathed with galvanized iron. Although the designer is unknown, the statement is commendable; the silhouette recalls, in sequence, the tower and spire of Saint Mary-le-Bow by Sir Christopher Wren. Indeed, although it is not so finely detailed as Wren's elevation, it remains an imaginative solution.

To the east of the cathedral is the Saint Francis Xavier Library (IN-75), built in 1840. The first library building constructed in Indiana, it now contains 5,000 books, many of which were published before 1800 and some even prior to 1700. The one-story, three-bay brick building, on a high base, is terminated by a hipped roof. It is a well-proportioned building in the Classical Revival style. With the Priests' House, built c. 1840 (IN-76), the three structures, in alignment, form an interesting composition. A HABS tean returned in 1970 to finish the recording of this complex, which also includes the Saint Rose Chapel (IN-74).

Numerous churches in Indiana were designed in the Greek Revival style. One of the finest expressions of the style is the Second Presbyterian Church (IN-15) in Madison, built in 1834–35 by the architect Edwin J. Peck. It is a one-story structure on a raised platform with a pseudo-octastyle temple front with Doric pilasters flanking two freestanding fluted Doric columns. The triglyphs and pediment are finely detailed and the facade is well proportioned. Now the Historic Madison Auditorium, used for concerts, conferences, and exhibitions, it is an excellent example of adaptive use for a historic structure.

Christ Episcopal Church (IN-3), grandly sited on the northeast quadrant of Monument Circle in Indianapolis, is a mature interpretation of the English Gothic parish church. Christ Church was not the first example of the Gothic Revival to be built in Indiana, but it certainly was, and remains today, a fine statement—although it is unfortunately now dominated by large-scale commercial buildings. The structure's rough-faced ashlar walls pierced by lancet arched openings were built in 1857; the tall spire was not built until 1869. The architect was William Tinsley (1804–1885), who was born in Clonmel, Ireland. Tinsley's father, grandfather, and great-grandfather were builders, and at the age of sixteen he was working with his father, Thomas, and his older brother, John, in the family construction business. While still in his twenties, he met James Pain, Jr., an architect who had studied under Sir John Nash, the eminent British architect. Tinsley built several buildings designed in the Gothic mode by Thomas Pain, Jr.[3]

For Christ Church Tinsley employed a traditional cruciform plan with polyfoil apse and slightly projecting transept. The spacious interior is defined by hammerbeam king-post trusses. "The wooden members spring from stone corbels, a favorite Tinsley device."[4] The tall, narrow lancet windows of the facade and transept walls and the trefoiled cusped bull's eye openings are filled with stained glass that gives an interesting luminous quality to the spacious interior. In 1900, sympathetic modifications included the addition of a wooden south porch, rood screen, and reredos. Indiana has scores of churches built in the Gothic Revival style; many are larger and more monumental than Christ Church in Indianapolis, but few are more strategically situated or finely detailed.

The sole commercial structure surveyed in the first year was the Richmond City Market (IN-14). James M. Smith designed this simple, utilitarian shed with gable roof as a single open space 100′ long by 24′ wide with a 6′ over-hang. Built in 1855, the structure was demolished c. 1965.

In contrast to the fate of the Richmond City Market, the second St. Joseph County Courthouse (IN-12) in South Bend is still in active use today by the Northern Indiana Historical Society. Built in 1854, the Classical Revival–style building is attributed to John Mills Van Osdel (1811–1891), the first architect to practice in Chicago. The building was moved to its present site in 1897 when the latest, or third, courthouse was placed in service.

The former courthouse, headquarters and museum for the Northern Indiana Historical Society since 1907, is a two-story building on a podium, expressed as a Roman Prostyle Temple, with a

4

hexastyle colonnade. The six columns are unevenly spaced: those at the end are closely spaced, but the others have a wide intercolumniation. The column caps are pseudo-Corinthian; the angle of the raking cornice is acute, but well detailed and interesting. The cupola that surmounts the simple, low gable roof is imposing, its height equal to the height of the building. The stepped, staged cupola is square in plan and is enhanced by diagonally projected corner pilasters, entablatures, and scroll brackets. The whole is capped by a polyfoil dome with a weather vane. The result is a unique and interesting combination of Classical Revival elements.

Similar imaginative variations in the combination of classical elements were also documented for important residences in different areas of the state. The Willard Carpenter House (IN-11) in Evansville, built in 1848, has a two-and-a-half-story main block that is austere but well proportioned, with a hipped roof and a monitor. The entablature is extremely tall and the frieze becomes an attic band with large horizontal windows. In the Ewing House (IN-10) in Fort Wayne, built in 1854 and demolished in 1963, a similar window system is employed on the front and rear elevations and at the corners of the end elevations. A gable roof terminates the Fort Wayne example. The windowed frieze and the two-story wooden porches on the two-story ell at the rear of the Carpenter House are elements that would often be employed in later Italianate- and Second Empire-style residences.

The David Macy House (IN-2) in Indianapolis was an example of the early Italianate style, which employed details from previous revival styles. Built in 1853, almost ten years after the Carpenter House, the Macy House nonetheless was given the earlier gable roof with individually splayed chimneys and horizontal windows in the frieze. However, the simple rectangular two-story building was terminated by an elaborately bracketed cornice. The boldly projecting eaves with a deep bracketed cornice were hallmark features of the Italianate style. In this instance, the relief-and-shadow effect was further heightened by the contrast established between the alternating wooden rosette panels and glazed openings in the frieze. The projecting three-sided bay on the south elevation and ornamental iron fencing were fine details that enriched the composition.

The Swinney Homestead (IN-6) in Fort Wayne was originally a one-and-a-half-story dwelling. Built in 1844 by Colonel Thomas W. Swinney, the proportions and details of the first-floor windows would seem to suggest that the initial house was based on traditional Classical Revival forms, possibly even a very simple Federal Revival. Remodeled and enlarged in 1855 by the addition of a second story and a servants' wing, the house has a "Swiss Chalet" character in the later detailing. The drawings of the house document the existing fabric and do not include a "restoration" scheme for the original configuration of the building. Archaeological investigation and analysis of a building was not included in the original HABS documentation projects. It was only after years of experience and training that the National Park Service, under the leadership of Charles Peterson, FAIA, of Philadelphia, introduced this element into recent projects.

Two of the structures surveyed in the first year were not buildings, but engineering structures. The Whitewater Canal Aqueduct (IN-20) over Duck Creek at Metamora, in Franklin County, was built in 1846. The Whitewater Canal linking Hagerstown, Indiana, and Cincinnati, Ohio, ceased to operate after the Civil War. However, a portion of the channel at Metamora was retained to operate a water-powered mill. In 1946, the aqueduct was dismantled and rebuilt, using some of the original timbers. The large replacement timbers came from Kentucky. The aqueduct, a part of the Whitewater Canal State Monument, is the only known covered wooden structure of this type in the United States.

At one time there were over four hundred covered bridges in the state, of which approximately one hundred survive.[5] Archibald Kennedy and his sons, Emmett L. and Charles R., headquartered in Rushville, were responsible for the construction of fifty-six covered bridges. Archibald, the public relations man who secured the commissions, retired in 1883 when he was elected a state senator. Emmett, who supervised construction, was building covered bridges as late as 1916, because of the steel shortage during World War I. In fact, prior to his death at the age of ninety in 1938, he and his brother, who had become a lawyer, were already repairing and refurbishing their earlier covered bridges that were even then considered landmarks. Thus it is not surprising that (IN-1) was a covered bridge.

The Kennedy Covered Bridge (IN-1), built in 1880 by Emmett L. and C. F. Kennedy, was located one mile east of Rushville on State Route 44 spanning the Flat Rock River. The 165'9" span, Burr arch structure, was the first covered bridge designed by the Kennedys to employ a wide center roadway flanked by pedestrian walkways.

A similar tripartite expression was used by the Kennedys in the construction of three other covered bridges situated near urban areas.[6] These four Kennedy bridges had an airy character, since the outer faces of the walkways were open, with balustrades between the vertical members of the trusses. Even the massive arches could be visually experienced from the sides. Old photographs reveal that the walkways became covered promenades. The aesthetic trademarks of Kennedy covered bridges, however, were the end portals, which were arched openings with paired brackets at the projecting eaves. The paired brackets recalled one of the hallmarks of the Italianate architectural style. Italianate design elements were still being employed in the late nineteenth century by the Kennedys.

The initial selection of structures included two buildings in New Harmony, the most remarkable "colony" in Indiana. The Rappite Community House No. 2 (IN-5), built by George Rapp and his followers in 1816 as a dormitory for unmarried men, is a brick, two-and-a-half-story structure. Purchased in 1824, by Robert Owen for the Owenite Community, it was altered internally after 1830 to accommodate also a store and residence. Now a museum operated by the Indiana Department of Natural Resources, it also once housed the first Pestalozzian School in America, under the auspices of the Owenite Community.

The other building surveyed in New Harmony, the David Dale Owen House (IN-4), built in 1859, was in accordance with the philosophy expressed by Dr. Owen's father, Robert Dale Owen, in the book *Hints on Public Architecture* (New York, 1849). It is the most picturesque and certainly one of the finest examples of a Gothic Revival residence in Indiana. Dr. Owen, an eminent geologist, reportedly designed this combination residence and laboratory with the assistance of James Renwick, who had been selected by his own father to design the Smithsonian Institution.[7] The unique one-and-a-half-story brick house is exotically embellished with rich and varied fenestration, including round, triangular, and flat-headed windows, some with cast-iron window hoods. The pagoda-roofed cupola and roof cresting result in a playful silhouette. Numerous other Gothic-inspired details, such as the oriel windows and ornate cast-iron porch on the south elevation and the elaborate metalwork of the cornice, including a cast-iron gutter, enrich this fine example.

In contrast, the William Logan Cabin (IN-19), built in 1809, originally near Fairfield before its removal and partial reconstruction at the Treaty Line Museum, was a hewn-log, 27' × 19' two-story house with no exterior decoration other than the construction details themselves. The gable ends of the attic were enclosed with clapboard siding. Siding was also used on the kitchen addition of 1845. However, at no time was any attempt made to conceal the dovetailed corners of the massive 6" × 18" logs. The east end of the ground-floor room had a stone fireplace hearth surrounded by raised block paneling. The major exterior embellishment was the two-story porch that extended the full width of the entrance facade. The heavy chamfered and turned wooden posts had simple capitals atop the second-story posts, which were a variation on the Doric form of the Roman Classical Revival.

The other vernacular-style structure documented in the initial survey was called the "Ferry House" (IN-16). Located on the Ohio River between Walnut and Ferry Streets in Vevay, it was operated as an inn to service river travelers. It was built in 1811 by John Francis Dufour, one of the Swiss settlers who founded Vevay. The two-and-a-half-story fieldstone main block was joined to the one-and-a-half-story fieldstone kitchen by a two-story frame addition. The exterior walls of the main block were stuccoed. An exterior staircase provided access to the second-floor level. The building was demolished in 1962.

Of these twenty structures documented by the HABS program, only five have been lost to neglect, accidents, or development pressures. Even more remarkable is the fact that twelve of the structures have been maintained and are now open to the general public on a regular basis, either as historic sites or through normal operations. These initial buildings also established the standards for subsequent Indiana documentations, in terms of both the execution of the drawings and the quality of the buildings selected.

The James F. D. Lanier House (IN-23) in Madison was surveyed in 1936 and 1971. Designed by Francis Costigan, it was completed in 1844. It is, without question, one of the finest expressions of Greek Revival to have been built in Indiana, and it is a rival to all other examples of domestic architecture in the Greek mode in the Old Northwest Territory.

The massive brick two-and-a-half-story main block of the Lanier House is capped by a low-hipped parapet roof crowned with a huge central wooden octagonal cupola. On the east side of the main block is a lower kitchen and service wing with a mansard roof. The north facade is the more restrained of the two major elevations. Two-story attentuated pilasters divide the wall into three bays, the windows are framed with pilasters and entablatures, and the covered entrance porch is supported by columns with elegant Corinthian capitals. The south elevation, which overlooks the Ohio River and which is approached by a broad lawn, is the most majestic exterior feature of the house. The slender, freestanding, tetrastyle two-story colonnade in the Corinthian order carries a deep entablature, with a raking parapet that is embellished with Grecian-inspired ornament crafted from lead and wood with metal edges. Fine wrought-iron railings define the portico, the main exterior stairway, and the first-floor windows on the south elevation. The fenestration is identical to that of the north elevation. The frieze has round windows framed with carved trim that are centered above each bay in the main block of the house. The richly landscaped site provides an ideal setting for this magnificent residence.

The interior spaces on the first floor of the Lanier House are monumental and delicately detailed. The double parlors, on the west, are separated by sliding doors and deep wooden enframement with shoulders, egg-and-dart moldings, and handsome Ionic columns. Other interior trim and detailing, including the entablatures and ornamental Greek fret brackets on the stair stringers, are finely crafted. The magnificent open circular stairway, which is partially recessed, is top-lighted by a polyfoil skylight. The circular stairway became a trademark of Costigan interiors.[8] The Lanier House is well preserved and is operated as a house museum by the Indiana Department of Natural Resources, Division of Museums and Memorials.

Another impressive design by Costigan is the Charles E. Shrewsbury House (IN-8), also at Madison, which was completed two years after the Lanier House. As with the Lanier House, Costigan employed a central hall plan and expressed it as a two-and-a-half-story form with a low-hipped roof. The exterior brick mass is well proportioned with brick pilasters at the corners. Horizontal windows in the frieze are similar to those later employed in the Carpenter House in Evansville. The ironwork is excellent; however, the unique feature of the residence is the freestanding central spiral stair, which is even more intriguing than the stair in the earlier Lanier House. The stairway is terminated by a low polyfoil dome that is top-lighted. The interior spaces are somewhat smaller than those in the Lanier House; however, they are equally well detailed, as shown by the paired Corinthian columns in the parlor. As Rexford Newcomb stated of Costigan, "had he designed nothing else, these two residences would secure his name to posterity."[9]

New Harmony was settled when George Rapp and his followers purchased 30,000 acres of land in the Indiana Territory on the Wabash River, about forty miles north of its confluence with the Ohio River and one hundred miles downsteam from Vincennes. By 1817, some seven hundred of the flock had settled at the new site of Harmonie. Within a decade, eighty-two one-story houses, thirty-four two-story houses, four family rooming houses, two churches, two schools, a granary, a hospital, and at least fifty additional buildings were constructed.[10]

The documentation of the five sites recorded for New Harmony in 1940 was limited solely to exterior photographs, except for the Schnee House (IN-30), in which case detail photographs of the special Rappite construction techniques were taken while the building was being demolished. The house's similarity to the other Rappite buildings was due to the use of standardized parts and mass production. Timbers cut at the mill were marked with identification numbers to permit rapid and accurate construction. Braced frames had mortised joints, as did roof rafters and ceiling joists; the timbers were massive, and stresses and loads were transferred by the timbers; the tenons and locking pegs functioned only as connectors. Frame and masonry buildings were insulated with "Dutch biscuits," which were carefully placed in attic floors, rafters, and in the ceilings of the first floor to reduce sound transmission. The biscuits were a one-by-four, eighteen inches long and carefully wrapped with straw and mud; the ends of the one-by-four were tapered to fit into channels cut in the sides of the ceiling joists.

After installation, the top of the biscuit layer was covered with clay while the ceiling plaster was put directly on the underneath side of this fireproof layer.[11] In framed houses, the space between the exterior clapboard siding and the interior plastered surface was filled with a nogging of soft-baked, or sun-baked, bricks laid in clay. Even though their tools were primitive and their natural resources limited, the Harmonists designed and constructed a series of buildings that were more than equal to any other buildings then under construction in Indiana.

In 1824, the Rappites sold their properties to Robert Owen, the ambitious English social reformer, and the name of the community was changed to New Harmony. The Rappites returned to Pennsylvania and established a new community at Economy. The Indiana community continued for a time to be a significant scientific and cultural center, but the Owenites made, at most, a modest impression on the architectural heritage of New Harmony.

The second group of structures surveyed was quite limited in number and scope of documentation. Of the last eighteen buildings recorded prior to World War II, measured drawings were made for seven sites during 1936, ten photographs were taken in 1936 at Conner Prairie Pioneer Settlement (IN-40, 44, 45, 46, 47), and in 1940 fourteen photographs were taken at New Harmony.

In addition to those made of the Lanier House, measured drawings were made of the Brown-Augustine House (IN-21) in the vicinity of New Carlisle. Built c. 1834 by Henry Brown, it was a fine house in the Western Reserve manner. An unusual feature was the false chimney on the west wing that balanced the operational chimney on the east wing, thus maintaining the symmetry of the Greek Revival style of this house. The house unfortunately burned in the 1950s. Drawings were made also of the Vinton-Pierce House (IN-24) in Indianapolis, designed by architect Joseph Curzon and built c. 1860. The two-and-a-half-story brick Italianate-style house was demolished in the late 1960s. These two structures were the only buildings in the northern half of Indiana documented with measured drawings during the second phase of the prewar work.

Two of the seven buildings, the Ruter Chapel (IN-27) and the Ulysses P. Schenck House (IN-28), are located in Vevay. The remaining two sites were the Old Salem School (IN-25), built in 1824 in Salem, and the Old State Capitol (IN-26) in Corydon. The Old Salem School is presently operated as a historic house museum by the Washington County Historical Society. The Old State Capitol, built in 1816 as the Harrison County Courthouse, is now a museum operated by the Department of Natural Resources, Division of Museums and Memorials.

With these final drawings and photographic recording projects, the early years of HABS documentation in Indiana came to a close. However, the interest generated by these projects in the various cities and towns brought recognition and appreciation for many of Indiana's architecturally and historically significant structures.

Notes

1. Of the twenty-eight, the following made drawings contained in this catalog: H. Wilson Peterson, Vincennes; John R. Kelley, Richmond; Lloyd W. Larimore, Fort Wayne; Joseph Fallon, Fairfield; Howard Garns, Vevay; F. H. Gregg, Indianapolis; Edward Thole, Evansville; Malcome T. Meek, Fort Wayne; T. L. Steele, Indianapolis; E. Jack Wesley, New Harmony; Charles E. Bacon, Vincennes; Forrest West, South Bend; Earl O. Warweg, Newburgh; C. E. Bedan, Jeffersonville.

2. Talbot Hamlin, *Greek Revival Architecture in America* (New York, 1944; reprint 1964), p. 298.

3. J. D. Forbes, *Victorian Architect: The Life and Work of William Tinsley* (Bloomington, 1953), p. 3. Mr. Forbes' volume on Tinsley is still the finest single volume on a nineteenth-century architect practicing in Indiana.

4. Ibid., p. 93.

5. Richard S. Allen, "Covered Bridges of the Middle West" (Brattleboro, 1970), p. 55.

6. Circleville Bridge, on the south edge of Rushville; East Connersville Bridge; and Vine Street Bridge at Shelbyville. Unfortunately, all four bridges have been demolished.

7. Wilbur Peat, *Indiana Houses of the Nineteenth Century* (Indianapolis, 1969), p. 89.

8. Costigan probably designed the freestanding circular stairway in

the Schenck House at Vevay, a fine Greek Revival example designed by the competent local architect George H. Kyle.

9.Rexford Newcomb, *Architecture of the Old Northwest Territory* (Chicago, 1950), p. 85.

10. Don Blair, *Harmonist Construction* (Indianapolis, 1964), pp. 48–50.

11. Ibid., p. 54.

HABS in Indiana, 1955–1982: Recollections

H. Roll McLaughlin, FAIA

My personal involvement with HABS dates from the early 1950s, when I assisted architect Edward D. James, my employer, in the recording of historic structures in Indiana. Using Historic American Building Survey Inventory (HABSI) forms, we recorded many buildings on these single sheets. A more select group of buildings, judged on historic significance or architectural merit, were singled out for the more intensive HABS documentation through field investigation, measuring, photography, and historical research. My interest in the history of architecture and the preservation of historic buildings, however, goes back to early experiences as a child when I visited historic sites and buildings with my parents. At the time, I was probably more impressed with the famous people "who slept there" than with the buildings themselves, but such structures as Monticello, the White House, Mount Vernon, and the buildings at Williamsburg, because of early visits, stand out in my mind to this day.

As AIA preservation officer for the State of Indiana since 1957, Mr. James had been in charge of continuing the HABS Inventory of historic structures throughout Indiana. Mr. James' close friend and colleague in the HABS regional office in Chicago was Earl H. Reed, FAIA. A native Hoosier who lived in Chesterton, Indiana, Mr. Reed commuted daily to his Chicago office. In my mind, Ed James and Earl Reed were really responsible for reactivating the HABS program in Indiana. Mr. Reed at the time was national coordinator for HABS drawings and inventories and served as liaison with the AIA National Committee in Washington, the National Park Service, and the Library of Congress. In May 1958, some monies were made available to us from the National Park Service, Division of Archaeology and Historic Preservation, through the efforts of Charles E. Peterson, FAIA.

"Pete," founder of HABS, was an architect with the National Park Service from January 1929 until October 1962. From 1950 to 1954, he was the resident architect of the Independence National Historic Park project in Philadelphia and, from 1954 to 1962, the supervising architect of historic structures in the National Park Service Eastern Office of Design and Construction.

One of Mr. Peterson's main concerns was to interest young architects in the field of restoration. At that time, there was little or no interest in teaching the history of architecture in some of our colleges, let alone thinking in terms of restoration as a specialized practice. Mr. Peterson's persistence resulted in the establishment in 1964 of graduate studies in building preservation at Columbia University. This was the first course of its type in America that offered a master's degree. One of the more vocal leaders and ardent preservationists, Mr. Peterson prefers to be called an architect-restorationist and is known internationally for his expertise and experience in this specialized field. Through his early efforts in HABS, he has brought about an awareness, both in our schools of architecture and in our homes, that we must preserve the best of our architectural heritage.

Mr. Peterson was assisted by a young man in his office named James C. Massey. Mr. Massey served as liaison between the Indiana HABS activities and Mr. Peterson's office. He made numerous trips to Indiana, and I in turn traveled to Philadelphia to attend special seminars involving HABS procedures and technical workshops on restoration. An extensive restoration was then underway in Philadelphia, including Independence Hall, the Bishop White House, and work generally in the Society Hill area. Mr. Massey became chief of HABS, and our Indiana programs were all coordinated through him.

In 1958, a list of ten structures and two alternates not previously recorded in the earliest HABS surveys of the 1930s was drawn up, and Mr. James and I were given five each. Mr. James' list included four buildings in New Harmony—(IN-37), (IN-38), (IN-5), and (IN-43)—plus the Joseph Bailly Homestead, (IN-42) near Chesterton, Indiana, in Porter County, Calumet Region. My list was mixed, beginning with two houses in Indianapolis—the House of Twin Chimneys (IN-36) on Allisonville Road and the William Prosser House (IN-35) on East 10th Street, home of the first ornamental plaster contractor in Indianapolis and noted for its outstanding exterior stucco and interior plasterwork; the other three sites were scattered over the southeastern part of the state—the John Wright House (never surveyed) in Vevay, Francis Costigan's Residence (IN-87) in Madison, and several buildings in New Harmony. The two alternates chosen were the Rappite Community House No. 3 (IN-39) in New Harmony and the Huddleston House (IN-110) near Cambridge City. Mr. James and I signed two agreements to prepare and furnish the Indiana Historical Society with measured drawings and reports to be deposited ultimately through HABS in the Library of Congress. These joint agreements marked the first of several successful, cooperative efforts between the Indiana Historical Society and HABS to document our state's historic architecture. Charles Peterson met with us in Ed James' office in July 1958, along with Earl Reed of Chicago and Hubert Hawkins, then executive director of the Indiana Historical Society. This meeting, reported and photographed by the press, served as the kickoff for a concentrated HABS program in Indiana.

In addition to those of us on the steering committee, other members of the statewide HABS committee were appointed. Paul Frank Jernegan of Mishawaka and Juliet Peddle of Terre Haute were the AIA representatives from their respective areas of the state. Mr. John T. Windle, president of Historic Madison, Inc., was the representative from southern Indiana. The committee also included Wilbur D. Peat, director of the Indianapolis Museum of Art, and Edward Pierre, FAIA, a well-known Indianapolis architect.

The first concentrated effort to survey and record historic structures was conducted in New Harmony, Indiana, in 1958, during a long weekend, sponsored by Mr. James at his expense. Volunteers for the weekend survey trip were for the most part recruited from the James organization. When Mr. James asked for volunteers, as I recall, only two of us responded, so in typical army colonel fashion Mr. James announced to the others, "You, you, and you are volunteering." The team, as recorded in my files, included Norman R. Jeffries, John W. Carmack, Ray Casati, H. Joseph Portish, and Stephen James from our office, plus E. Roger Frey of Disciples of Christ National Headquarters in Indianapolis, Board of Church Extension, Architectural Division. All were advised by Mr. James that it would be a long, hardworking weekend. This was the first Indiana HABS team organized since the 1930s.

In New Harmony, our local contact was Don Blair, engineer and local historian. Mr. Blair acted as consultant and guide, and assisted in providing early photographs and other documents of historic value. Other important contacts in New Harmony included Mrs. Kenneth Owen, Miss Helen Elliott, and Mr. John Elliott. The survey work in New Harmony drew considerable attention. The Construction League of Indianapolis published an illustrated article on the work in the October 1958 issue of their magazine. Excellent press

HABS measuring party at New Harmony, September
1958. *Standing, left to right:* Edward D. James, Norman R.
Jeffries, Ray Casati, E. Roger Frey, John W. Carmack,
H. Joseph Portish, Stephen James.
Kneeling: H. Roll McLaughlin

coverage continued with a fine *Sunday Star Magazine* article by Lotus
Benning Stuart in late November, with photographs of the teams at
work. These articles plus others were very important in bringing
about an awareness of our architectural heritage and triggered a
program to educate Hoosiers as to the importance of HABS.

In 1960, I was appointed assistant preservation officer for Indiana under Mr. James, whose duties were far reaching in the field
of preservation. I was given the responsibility for continuing committee work, executing HABS Inventory forms, and surveying additional historic structures in Indiana for HABS. I recall on one occa-
sion a memo from Mr. James advising that I was not producing as
many completed HABSI forms as he expected and that, if I could
not, he would find someone who would. A public-relations program
was developed and regular talks were given in an effort further to
arouse the public through service clubs, civic organizations, high
schools, and colleges. The growing interest in preservation sparked
the attention of several civic leaders, especially Mr. Eli Lilly. Calvin S.

Hamilton, then executive director of the Department of Metropolitan Development for Marion County, called the first meeting of citizens believed to have interest in forming a nonprofit organization for the preservation of our architectural heritage. After several planning-committee meetings, it was determined that such an organization would be founded, and prospective charter members were solicited.

On September 30, 1960, the organization was finally incorporated and would be known as Historic Landmarks Foundation of Indiana (HLFI), with Eli Lilly and Herman Krannert as cochairmen. James E. Hoover of Eli Lilly & Company was elected president, with me as first vice-president, Harold Gossman as second vice-president, Richard E. Deer as secretary, and Linton G. Cox as treasurer. The first board of directors included Mrs. John Alexander, Allen W. Clowes, Edward D. James, Kurt Pantzer, Edward D. Pierre, and John R. Walsh. Since the HABS team had laid the groundwork and stimulated interest in the recording process, it seemed only natural that the first project proposed for Historic Landmarks Foundation was involvement in HABS activity.

As a result, a survey team was formed to investigate known historic property in Marion County and surrounding areas. Files on each of the buildings researched were established. Those structures originally surveyed were recorded through HABSI, and more than half were processed through HABS with drawings, photographs, and historic documentation. Unfortunately, several of the buildings in the early survey were razed long before the efforts of HLFI and allied groups were able to convince the owners of the buildings' significance. The first HLFI survey committee developed files on domestic architecture in areas such as Lockerbie Square, including the Joseph Staub House (IN-50), Woodruff Place (IN-67), Irvington with the Benton House (HABSI), homes in what are now known as the Old Northside and the Chatham-Arch historic districts, plus homes on North Meridian Street in the Meridian Street Preservation District. Commercial and public buildings that were fortunately recorded before they were razed included the old American National Bank (Old Federal Building) (HABSI), designed in 1856 and located at Pennsylvania and Market Streets), the Indiana National Bank (IN-62) at Washington and Virginia Avenue, the Maennerchor (IN-100) at North and Illinois Streets, the old Indianapolis Public Library (HABSI) at Meridian and Ohio, which also served as the Indianapolis school administration office for many years, and the Marion County Courthouse—all of which have since been destroyed. Despite the ardent efforts of Mr. James to save them, some

17

of the most important structures in our business community were lost. Through the efforts of HABS, they were at least recorded as significant contributions to the architectural history of Indianapolis.

A statement to the press by Mr. James on February 1, 1963, related his feelings:

> If an organization such as Historic Landmarks Foundation had been formed five or ten years ago, we could have saved buildings that in my opinion are the finest examples of early architecture in Indianapolis. First among those destroyed is the Old Federal Building at Pennsylvania and Market Street. Sometime ago an opportunity was available to purchase this structure at a modest cost, with the stipulation that the building be used for public purposes. Unfortunately, there was not significant interest by others or by an organization such as HLFI to support my ideas for the future of this building. As a result, the steel ball and wrecking bar have now reduced the building to rubble.
>
> All attempts to save this structure failing, our last alternative was to measure, photograph, and record the building for a permanent resting place in the files of the Library of Congress, through the cooperation of HABS. I have taken the responsibility of using my own organization to perform this service at a cost exceeding $5,000. Members of my staff worked for several months prior to the demolition of the structure compiling records, taking field measurements and photographs, from which final drawings could be drafted. All the records will be processed through the Department of the Interior, National Park Service, HABS.
>
> It is my hope that now and in the future Historic Landmarks Foundation can take over the work of a few individuals and arouse the community to its responsibility and to its architectural heritage.

In July 1962, Mr. James was appointed vice-chairman of the National AIA Committee of Preservation of Historic Buildings, and soon thereafter I received an appointment as preservation officer for the Indiana Society of Architects. HABS and HABSI activity was continued throughout the 1960s largely by Mr. James, members of the state committee, and me as time permitted. Following Mr. James' retirement in 1966, I succeeded him on the HABS advisory board until 1972. Serving during the same period on the AIA National Committee for Historic Preservation, I became chairman in 1970. Good liaison was established for Indiana HABS activities. In a joint-venture agreement with AIA, the National Trust, the Library of Congress, and the National Park Service, Division of Archaeology and Historic Preservation, HABS was now well established. The HABS Inventory (HABSI) was dropped following the National Historic Preservation Act of 1966, which established the National Register of Historic Places.

In February 1963, Historic Landmarks Foundation brought to Indianapolis as a guest speaker Helen Duprey Bullock, director of the Department of Information, National Trust for Historic Preservation. Mrs. Bullock's presentation, further stimulating the interest of Indiana preservationists, helped bring about a more cooperative attitude and joint ventures between HLFI, the National Trust, the AIA, HABS, and the Library of Congress.

Historic Landmarks Foundation for several years operated with officers volunteering their services until we restored the Morris-Butler House at 1204 North Park Avenue. In the late 1960s, a room over the kitchen became the first office of HLFI, with Robert C. Braun as executive director. Several years later, acquisition of the Old Waiting Station (IN-56) at the entrance to Crown Hill Cemetery provided the additional space required for the expanding organization, with J. Reid Williamson, Jr., named executive director in 1974.

During the late 1960s and early 1970s, Historic Landmarks Foundation sponsored several HABS summer programs in Indiana. In 1970, HLFI made a grant of $10,000 to match funds of the National Park Service for a summer survey program in Marion County using architectural students for survey work under the leadership of Professor David Hermansen of Ball State University, College of Architecture and Planning, with Professor Wesley Shank of Iowa State University, historian. Some nine buildings in the Indianapolis area were surveyed and measured, with sixteen more recorded with photographs and written data (IN-49–73). The nine included structures in Lockerbie Square, the Morris-Butler House (IN-52), and the Benjamin Harrison Home (IN-53).

In 1971, another grant was provided by HLFI together with one from Historic Madison to match National Park Service money to measure historic structures in the Madison area. Seven buildings were surveyed and measured, with eight others recorded and historically documented (IN-82–92). Professor Melvin Rotsch of Texas A & M University led the student team; Phillip Dole of the University of Oregon provided the historic reports.

The third project, for eastern Indiana, was undertaken in 1974 with a grant from both HLFI and the Indiana Historical Society. This recording program covered several buildings in both Wayne and Fayette counties, including Huddleston House (IN-110) on the Old National Road, now a museum property and the eastern regional office of Historic Landmarks Foundation. The recording team of architectural students was supervised by Professor Mort

Karp of the University of Arkansas. Eight structures were measured and drawn while nine more were documented (IN-102–120) by the project historian, Professor Robert Bruegmann of the University of Pennsylvania.

In 1981, Samuel A. Roberson, architectural historian, was engaged to do additional research, to bring the files up to date, and to revise the 1971 catalog prepared by William P. Thompson to include all structures recorded by HABS in Indiana since 1933.

It is most fitting that publication of the Indiana HABS catalog take place in 1983, the fiftieth anniversary of HABS' founding. Significant also is the award for the best set of measured drawings donated to HABS by a student of architecture. Although the HABS program is now well established as a required course in most of our colleges of architecture, there are still those of us "Ole Timers" who will not completely give up. To prove our dedication and continuing support, we formed a steering committee comprised of HABS friends and advisers emeritus.

In May 1973, John Poppeliers, then chief of HABS, called a meeting in Washington, D.C., to discuss plans to organize the group that is now known as Friends of HABS. The steering committee selected three of us to address letters to past board members, staff, students, and former survey team members inviting their participation. The response was immediately positive, and Friends of HABS was officially founded, commemorating HABS' fortieth year. Now, ten years later, as we celebrate the fiftieth year of HABS, we see it as a national asset of superior value.

The Historic American Buildings Survey has proved to be the major advancement in the teaching of architectural history and craftsmanship. Its lessons have provided the students of our profession a new and exciting insight into the built environment. For those of us associated with HABS, there is little doubt that its discoveries have made us even more aware of our great architectural heritage and of our responsibility to document and preserve it for future generations.

The HABS Indiana Catalog

Bloomington   **Monroe County (53)**

Wylie, Andrew, House (IN-41), NE. corner Second and Lincoln Sts.
Historic house museum of Indiana University. Brick, L-shaped, 32′
(three-bay front) × 40′ main block, 34′ × 21′ side wing, two stories,
gable roofs with balustrade on upper slope of main block, two-story
gallery on wing. Built 1835 for Andrew Wylie, first president of Indiana University; George Troop and John McDonald, builders. 4
ext. photos (1952, 1955), 1 photocopy of floor plans (n.d.); 4 data
pages (1959, 1961). NR

Cambridge City   **Wayne County (89)**

Conklin House (IN-98), 302 E. Main St. (U.S. Rt. 40), SE. corner E.
Main St. and N. Lincoln Dr. Brick, originally U-shaped on first floor
with shop in W. wing, residence in E. wing, delivery court between
wings (now enclosed for kitchen); second floor had large workroom
over court; 52′ (five-bay front) × 58′ (six bays), two-and-a-half
stories, combination hipped and gable roof, recessed two-story entry
with two columns *in antis* at each floor, recessed balcony above rear
entrance; c. 1850 scroll-work porch leads to garden on E.; one-story
addition (now garage) at SE. corner; central stairhall; original carved
interior trim remains; Greek Revival style. Built c. 1839–40 for Benjamin Conklin, merchant and land speculator; restored 1950s. 10
sheets (1974, including plot plan, plans, elevations, section, details);
8 ext. photos (1975), 3 int. photos (1975), photocopy of Cambridge
City map (1871), photocopy of portrait of Benjamin Conklin (n.d.);
10 data pages (1974). NR

Centerville   **Wayne County (89)**

Julian, Judge Jacob, House (Gov. Oliver P. Morton House) (IN-102),
SE. corner W. Main St. (U.S. Rt. 40) and Willow Grove Rd. Brick,

Conklin House, north elevation

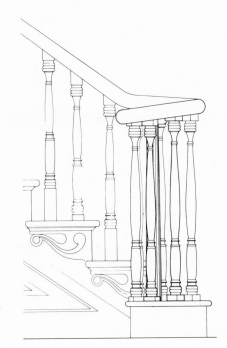

Conklin House, stair detail

30'9" (three-bay front) × 78' (including rear additions), two stories with slightly lower rear block and one-story ell, gable roofs, side hall plan, simple Greek Revival details. Built 1847–48 by Judge Jacob Julian; purchased 1856 by Oliver P. Morton, Indiana's Civil War governor (1861–66) and later U.S. senator (1867–77); sold to Judge William Peele in 1863; windows added to W. wall in 1920s; original interior trim altered or removed. Owned and maintained by Historic Centerville, Inc. Gov. Morton was a founder of the Republican Party; because of Democratic opposition, he ran the state without a legislature during the Civil War and borrowed money to pay and equip soldiers. 3 ext. photos (1975), 3 int. photos (1975); 8 data pages (1974). NR

Lantz House

Lantz House (IN-103), 214 W. Main St. (U.S. Rt. 40). Brick, U-shaped complex of residence and shop, each with ell; units are joined by a connecting section with a one-story arch that opens into the court-yard between the ells; 60'3" (three-bay shop, three-bay house, one-bay connector) × 48'4", two stories, gable roofs, Federal style; house has side hall plan, shop has open plan. House probably built c. 1835 for Daniel Lantz, a wagon maker; rear ell of house and shop may be c. 1820; owned by Lantz family until 1927; restored 1963–69. Excellent example of the unique "Centerville arch"—two adjacent row houses joined by a vehicular arch; six other examples exist in Centerville. 8 sheets (1972, including plot plan, plans, elevations, sections, details); 8 ext. photos (1975), 4 int. photos (1975); 11 data pages (1974). NR (Centerville Historic District)

Mansion House (IN-104), 214 E. Main St. (U.S. Rt. 40). Museum of Wayne County Historical Society. Brick, 32'6" (four-bay front) × 71'6" (including rear one-story kitchen ell), three stories, gable roof with paired brackets, side hall plan, two secondary entrances on E. and W. with pent hoods on elongated brackets, open porch along E. side of ell. Built 1837 for innkeeper Henry Rowan; bracketed cornice added mid-19th C.; W. half of building supposedly demolished 1870s; interior alterations; restored 1960s. Fine example of an inn that served travelers on the National Road (U.S. Rt. 40); scene of several early temperance raids. 8 sheets (1972, including plans, elevations, section); 7 ext. photos (1975), 2 int. photos (1975); 11 data pages (1974). NR (Centerville Historic District)

Masonic Hall. See Wayne County Warden's House and Jail (IN-105), Centerville.

Morton, Gov. Oliver P., House. See Judge Jacob Julian House (IN-102), Centerville.

Wayne County Warden's House and Jail (now Masonic Hall) (IN-105), 126 E. Main St. (U.S. Rt. 40). Brick with stone trim, 70' (four-bay front) × 33' (two bays), two-and-a-half stories on raised limestone basement, hipped roof, bracketed modillion cornice with attic frieze windows, slightly projecting gabled entrance pavilion, corner quoins, stone belt courses, double windows with round-arched or segmental arched heads and stone trim, elaborate cast-iron stairs to main arched entrance, Italianate style. Built 1867; Isaac Hodgson, architect; originally T-shaped structure with three-bay residence in front and 20-cell jail wing extending to rear; jail wing moved to Richmond 1873 when county seat transferred; E. bay added and interior altered 1924 when building became Masonic Hall. 8 ext. photos (1975); 9 data pages (1974). NR (Centerville Historic District).

Centerville Vicinity   **Fayette County (21)**

Ranck Round Barn (IN-106). See Waterloo Vicinity.

Augsburg Swensk Skola (Burstrom Chapel) (IN-48). See Porter Vicinity.

Bailly, Joseph, Homestead (IN-42). See Porter Vicinity.

Columbus   **Bartholomew County (3)**

Zaharako's Confectionary (IN-77), 329 Washington St. Commercial building with living quarters above and shop below; an extravagant and unaltered example of an early 19th C. soda fountain, still operated by the same family; long, narrow plan with pressed-tin ceiling and mirror-paneled walls; front part of shop contains candy display, sales area, and soda fountain; two Mexican onyx soda fountains purchased in 1905 from St. Louis World's Fair; barback of mahogany, mirrors, onyx, and stained-glass added 1911; also added was a 40' counter of onyx and Italian marble that features a Tiffany-style light fixture; counter area divided from seating area in rear by a spindle-work screen; screen and oak woodwork by Hege and Kendall Milling Co.; at rear of store is a mechanical pipe organ with full orchestration made by M. Welte of Frieburg, Germany, installed in 1908; stainless-steel luncheonette counter added 1949; facade altered 1959 after damage by runaway auto. 8 int. photos (1974).

Connersville   **Fayette County (21)**

Canal House (IN-107), 111 E. 4th St., SE. corner 4th St. and Central Ave. Brick, 30'11" (three-bay front) × 57'5" (including one-story rear addition), two stories, gable roof, side hall plan, temple-form Greek Revival style, pedimented portico with four fluted Doric columns, paired brick pilasters on sides, principal first-floor rooms separated by two brick storage vaults with iron-plate doors. Built c. 1843 as headquarters of Whitewater Valley Canal Co., a private company that took over development of Whitewater Canal from the state in 1842; later became a residence; balcony under portico and fireplaces in E. rooms added 1930s by Congressman and Mrs. Finley Gray; further alterations 1948 when building became VFW Hall; under restoration as museum by Historic Connersville, Inc. 9 sheets (1974, including plans, elevations, section); 4 ext. photos (1975), 2 int. photos (1975), 3 int. photocopies (1930s); 10 data pages (1974). NR

Zaharako's Confectionary, barback

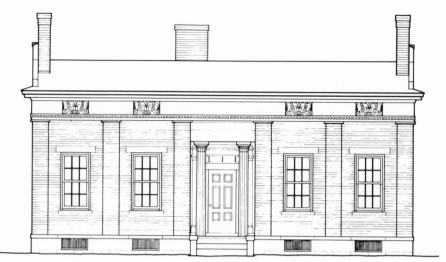

Gray House, west elevation

Connersville Vicinity   Fayette County (21)

Gray House (IN-108), E. side County Rd. 650, 2 mi. S. of State Rt. 44,
9 mi. SW. of Connersville. Brick, T-shaped, 43' (five-bay front) ×
57' (not including frame garage at rear of wing), one-and-a-half
stories with one-story wing, low gable roof, recessed entry with two
fluted Doric columns *in antis,* brick pilasters between bays, frieze
windows with ornamental iron grilles, modified central hall plan;
much original interior trim remains, including built-in cabinet and
secretary flanking S. parlor fireplace; Greek Revival style. Probably
built between 1836 and 1846 by Hugh Gray; traditionally attributed
to a New York architect named Smith; minor interior alterations. A
small, but architecturally sophisticated, farmhouse. A similar house
exists a few miles away. 6 sheets (1974, including plans, elevations); 8
ext. photos (1975), 4 int. photos (1975); 8 data pages (1974); HABSI
form (1970).

Corydon   Harrison County (31)

Old State Capitol (IN-26), State Rt. 135, one block N. of intersection
State Rt. 62. Museum of the State of Indiana. Native blue limestone,
coursed rubble masonry, 40' (three-bay front) × 40', two stories,
high-pitched roof, large octagonal louvered cupola, door enframement of fluted pilasters supporting entablature, double door and

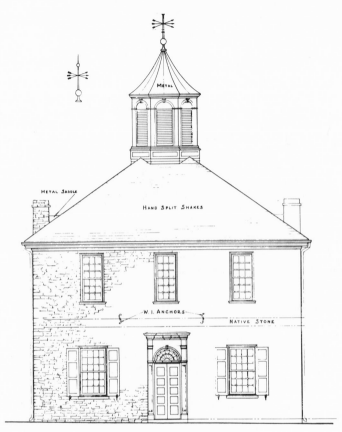

Old State Capitol, west elevation

fanlight recessed in paneled reveal. Built 1816 by Harrison County and lent to new state government for use as capitol; restored 1929; served as capitol until 1825 when Indianapolis became seat of state government. 13 sheets (1936, including plans, elevations, section, details); 5 ext. photos (1940), 1 int. photo (1940). NR (Corydon Historic District)

Dunlapsville   **Union County (81)**

Logan, William, Cabin (IN-19). See Fairfield Vicinity.

28

Carpenter, Willard, House (IN-11), 405 Carpenter St. Brick, 56' (five-bay front) × 52' (five bays), two-and-a-half-story main block, 21' × 40' two-story kitchen ell with two-story wooden porches on E. and W. sides; roof of main block is hipped; S. (main) entry has wooden pilaster enframement and one-story two-pier porch; wooden cornice, attic band with horizontal windows, severe Greek Revival design, central hall plan with stair in NE. side hall, plaster cornice and ceiling ornament, one-story laundry building at rear demolished after 1934. Built 1848 for Willard Carpenter, businessman and philanthropist; Gottlieb Bippus, carpenter. Adapted for use as offices. 15 sheets (1934, including plans, elevations, details); 2 ext. photos (1934); 1 data page (1934). NR

Willard Carpenter House, west elevation

Logan, William, Cabin (IN-19), originally 100 yds. W. of State Rt. 101 and 300 yds. S. of Brier Cemetery Rd., moved to Treaty Line Museum, Dunlapsville, Union County. Hewn log, 27' × 19', two stories, two-story porch; one-story frame kitchen addition, 16' × 19'; one-story porches at E. and W. now destroyed; gable roofs; of original two massive stone end chimneys, only one remains. Built 1809 by William Logan; kitchen added c. 1845; cabin dismantled c. 1967 and

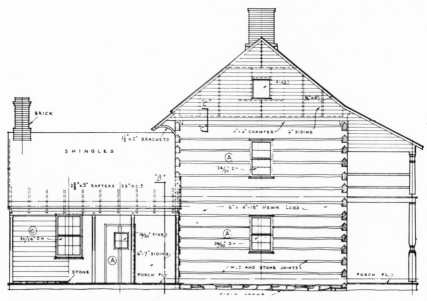

William Logan Cabin, west elevation

reerected in Treaty Line Museum. 8 sheets (1934, including plans, elevations, section, details); 4 ext. photos (1934); 1 data page (1934).

Fort Wayne   Allen County (2)

Ewing, William G., House (IN-10), NW. corner Ewing and Berry Sts. Brick, 50' (five-bay front) × 79' (including rear ell), two-and-a-half stories with dressed-stone basement, gable roof with tin sheeting and deck along ridge, wide wooden cornice containing attic windows, metal balcony along S. elevation at second floor, stone two-column Doric entrance portico, transitional Greek Revival style, central hall plan, spiral staircase. Built 1854 by William G. Ewing; demolished c. 1963. 17 sheets (1934, including plans, elevations, section, details, one sheet on rear outbuilding); 2 ext. photos (1934), 2 int. photos (1934); 2 data pages (1934).

Swinney, Col. Thomas W., House (Swinney Homestead) (IN-6), 1424 W. Jefferson St., in Swinney Park. Allen County–Fort Wayne Historical Museum. Brick, 48' (five-bay front) × 38', two-and-a-half stories, gable roof with large central wall dormers at E. and W., bracketed eaves, shingle trim on gables and dormers, wooden Stick-style porch on E. elevation, central hall plan. Built 1844 as story-and-a-half dwelling by Col. Thomas W. Swinney; remodeled 1885 by addition of second story and servants' wing; 1844 woodwork remains on first floor. 10 sheets (1934, including plans, elevations, sections, details); 2 ext. photos (1934), 1 int. photo (1934); 2 data pages (1934).

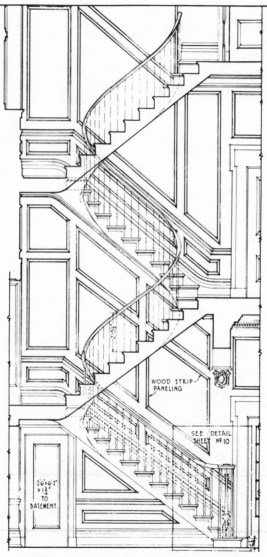

William G. Ewing House, stair section

Col. Thomas W. Swinney House, east elevation

Fort Wayne Vicinity   **Allen County (2)**

Aboite Township District School No. 5 (IN-155), intersection Aboite Center and Homestead Rds. Brick, limestone foundation, 34′ (five-bay front) × 27′ (two bays). One story, hipped roof, projecting gabled entry vestibule with flanking cloak room, recessed wall panels with segmental rowlock arches, open bell cupola above entry pavilion. Built 1893. Single schoolroom plan common to late 19th C. schools of this type. 5 sheets (n.d., including site plan, plan, elevations).

Pleasant Township School (IN-78), SW. corner Smith and Ferguson Rds., 1 mi. W. of Fort Wayne Municipal Airport, 7 mi. S. of Fort Wayne Civic Center. Brick, 38′6″ (five-bay front) × 38′, limestone foundation, one story, hipped slate roof with three intersecting gables, bell cot, projecting entrance vestibule, segmental arched windows, bull's eye windows in gables, wooden cornice with small brackets, open bell cupola, open plan. Built 1898 to serve Pleasant Township School District No. 3; used for storage since 1939. Typical late 19th C. rural school building. 7 sheets (1972, including site plan, plan, elevations, section, details); 3 data pages (1972).

Aboite Township District School No. 5, south elevation

Fountain City   **Wayne County (89)**

Coffin, Levi, House (IN-79), 115 N. Main St., SE. corner U.S. Rt. 27
and Mill St. Historic house museum of Levi Coffin House Association. Brick, L-shaped, 38′8″ (five-bay front) × 50′2″, two-and-a-half
stories, gable roof on main house, shed roof on ell, one-story brick
woodshed at rear of ell added c. 1967 to replace original frame ell
destroyed early 20th C., central hall plan; original interior woodwork of yellow poplar and tulipwood remains. Built 1839 for Levi
Coffin, known as "president" of the Underground Railroad for his
efforts to aid runaway slaves; house was a principal Underground
Railroad depot; small room under eaves of ell reputed to be a hiding
place for slaves; house restored 1967–70. 10 sheets (1971, including
site plan, plans, elevations, section, details); HABSI form (1958).
NHL NR

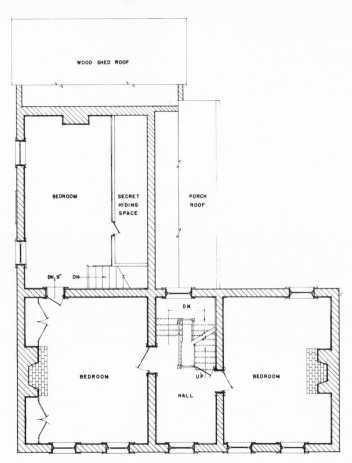

Levi Coffin House, second-floor plan

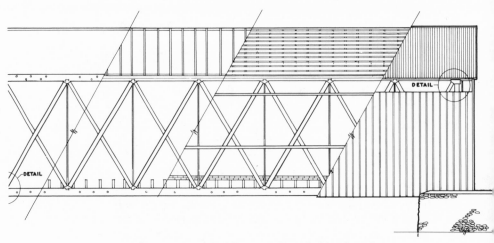

Ceylon Covered Bridge, portion of side elevation

Ceylon Covered Bridge (IN-156), County Rd. 950, 0.9 mi. E. of U.S. Rt. 27. Frame with vertical siding, stone piers, approx. 140' long, single span, Howe trusses. Built c. 1860; builder unknown. Last covered bridge spanning the Wabash River; now within 41-acre Limberlost Park. 7 sheets (n.d., including site plan, plans, elevations, sections, details).

House of Chief Richardville (Jean Baptiste Richardville Home) (IN-157), SW. corner junction U.S. Rt. 20 and State Rt. 9. Frame with clapboarding, main block 55' (three-bay front) × 42'; one-and-a-half-story rear ell is an earlier structure; ell forms one-story porch on N. side; main facade has recessed entry with entablature and engaged Doric pilasters; side hall plan; Greek Revival. Built 1833. Within a 10–sq. mi. Indian reserve, house was home of the last chief of the Miamis, Pe-she-wah, Jean Baptiste Richardville, nephew of Chief Little Turtle. 10 sheets (n.d., including plans, elevations, section, details); 2 ext. photos (1971); 15 data pages (1971).

Academy of Music. See Maennerchor Building (IN-100), Indianapolis.

Allison, James A., House ("Riverdale") (IN-68), 3200 Cold Spring Rd., now on Marian College campus. Reinforced concrete with brick veneer, carved stone trim, two-and-a-half stories with raised stone basement exposed on N., hipped roof, porte cochere, luxurious interior with carved mahogany woodwork, marble mantels, marble and parquet floors; wall finishes are leather, silk, and velour; rooms originally included conservatory with pipe organ, aviary with stained-glass roof, and heated swimming pool. Complex of garage, power plant, and servants' quarters S. of house. Built 1911–14; H. L. Bass, architect. James Allison manufactured the first efficient automobile headlight and was a founder of the Indianapolis Motor Speedway. 1 ext. photo (c. 1916), 1 ext. photo (1970), 10 int. photos (c. 1916); 6 data pages (1977); HABSI form (1963). NR

Arsenal Technical High School. See U.S. Arsenal, Arsenal Building (IN-66), Indianapolis.

Athenaeum, The. See Das Deutsche Haus (IN-63), Indianapolis.

Ayres, L. S., Company Warehouse Annex. See Elliott's Block (IN-60), Indianapolis.

Bates-Hendricks House (IN-64), 1526 S. New Jersey St. Brick, L-shaped, 46' × 80', two stories, segmental arched windows and doors, gable roofs, bracketed cornice, Italianate style. Built in three sections; S. block probably erected c. 1860; orientation changed, three-and-a-half-story mansard entrance tower and N. addition built c. 1865; service wing extended c. 1875. Home of Thomas A. Hendricks, Indiana governor and U.S. vice president under Grover Cleveland. 2 ext. photos (1970); 14 data pages (1971); HABSI form (1962). NR

Bates-Hendricks House

Christ (Episcopal) Church (IN-3), 131 Monument Circle, E. side N. Meridian St., at Monument Circle. Quarry-faced limestone ashlar, 47' × 140', cross plan with slightly projecting transepts, cross-gable roof, three-stage entrance tower at SW. corner, pentagonal apse, Gothic Revival style; interior has exposed hammerbeam king-post trusses, fine plate tracery, and colored glass. Built 1857–58; William Tinsley, architect; spire added 1869. Two-story stone parish house,

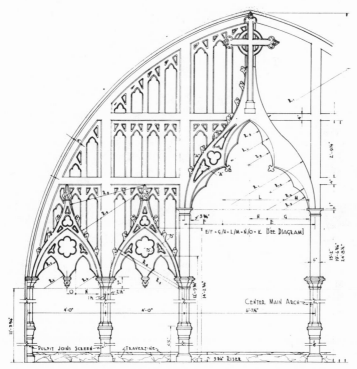

Christ (Episcopal) Church, rood screen, elevation

wooden S. porch, enlarged chancel, rood screen, and reredos all added 1900; W. and J. Lamb, architects. 18 sheets (1934, including plot plan, plans, elevations, section, details); 1 ext. photo (1934), 2 int. photos (1934); 5 data pages (1934); HABSI form (1958). NR

Cole Motor Car Company Factory (now Service Supply Co., Inc.) (IN-71), 730 E. Washington St. Reinforced concrete with glazed-brick facade, approx. 100' (three-bay front) × approx. 390' (eighteen bays), four stories, flat roof, three paired windows in each bay of facade; Cole emblem appears just below cornice in center of each bay; Commercial style with Art Deco details. Built 1910; major addition to rear 1911; E. and W. glass curtain wall now enclosed. One of the largest of the companies that made Indianapolis an automobile manufacturing center in the early 20th C. 1 ext. photo (1970); 4 data pages (1971).

Cornelius Printing Company. See Elliott's Block (IN-60), Indianapolis.

Cole Motor Car Company Factory

Crown Hill Cemetery, Chapel and Vault (IN-58), in Crown Hill Cemetery, opposite 34th St. Quarry-faced limestone, cruciform plan, approx. 65' (seven bays) × 50', gable roofs, two-story central chapel with crypts in one-story transepts; Gothic Revival details include dressed-stone buttresses, tracery, drop-arch doorway, paired blind arches, crocketed pinnacles; chapel has rib-vaulted ceiling. Built 1875–77; D. A. Bohlen, architect. Polygonal apse added 1917; D. A. Bohlen & Son, architects. Remodeled and storage vaults removed from crypts 1971; James Associates, architects. 7 ext. photos (1970), 3 int. photos (1970); 6 data pages (1971). NR (Crown Hill Cemetery)

Crown Hill Cemetery, Gateway (IN-57), 3402 Boulevard Pl., at E. entrance to cemetery. Smooth-finished limestone ashlar, three compound drop-arch openings with crocketed gables above, pinnacled buttresses separating arches, elaborately decorated iron gates. Built 1885; Adolf Scherrer, architect. Castellated porter's lodge added 1904 at S. side of gate; Vonnegut & Bohn, architects. 6 ext. photos (1970); 3 data pages (1971). NR (Crown Hill Cemetery)

Crown Hill Cemetery, Waiting Station (now Historic Landmarks Foundation of Indiana state offices) (IN-56), 3402 Boulevard Pl., at E. entrance to cemetery. Brick, limestone, and terra cotta trim,

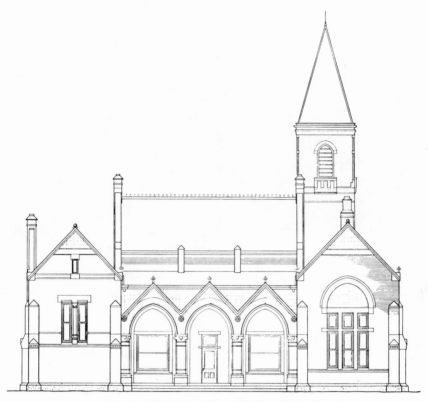

Crown Hill Cemetery, Waiting Station

U-shaped with triple-arched loggia joining legs of U, 76′ × 52′, three gabled units, shed roof over loggia, one story, three-stage square tower at NE. corner, hammerbeam ceilings and paneled wainscoting, carved wooden mantels, Gothic Revival style. Built 1885; Adolf Scherrer, architect. New vault added 1929. Restored as offices of Historic Landmarks Foundation of Indiana 1970–71; James Associates, architects. Originally built as a gathering place for funeral processions when cemetery was far from the city; later used as cemetery offices. 7 sheets (1971, including site plan, plans, elevations, section, details); 5 ext. photos (1970), 2 int. photos (1970); 14 data pages (1970–71). NR (Crown Hill Cemetery)

Das Deutsche Haus (now the Athenaeum) (IN-63), 401 E. Michigan St., at N. New Jersey St. Brick with stone trim, 190′ × 180′, roughly U-shaped with beer garden at rear. Built in two sections: E. wing in the German Romanesque style has large ornamental gables and

Das Deutsche Haus, architect's perspective

corner towers, basically two-and-a-half stories on raised stone basement; W. wing in Renaissance Revival style has banded masonry at
first floor, frontispiece terminates in large ornamental pediment at
hipped roof, wall of large glazed openings above arched loggia faces
garden. E. wing built 1892–93, W. wing built 1897–98; Vonnegut &
Bohn, architects for both wings. Building contains lounges, halls,
banquet rooms, and gymnasium; built as a German-American ath-
letic and social center by the Socialer Turnverein. 6 ext. photos
(1970), 9 int. photos (1970), photocopy of perspective (1898 or earlier), 1 ext. photocopy (1898), 4 int. photocopies (1898); 14 data
pages (1970–71). NR

Despa House (IN-55), 538 Lockerbie St. Brick, 24′9″ (three-bay front)
× 33′8″, one-and-a-half stories, gable roof perpendicular to street,
side hall plan, one-story brick and frame additions at rear. Built c.
1863; restored. Modest working-class house, typical of the Lockerbie
neighborhood. 8 sheets (1970, including plot plan, plans, elevations,
section, details); 3 data pages (1971). NR (Lockerbie Square)

Duesenberg Automobile Company Factory (IN-70), 1501 W. Washington,
SW. corner W. Washington and Harding Sts. Small factory building
on Harding St. is 15 bays long; large factory building on W. Wash-

ington St. is 24 bays long; both are one-story functional factory construction; steel frame, exterior brick walls, glass curtain wall window
openings, sloping roof with central monitor, open plan. Office building on W. Washington has reinforced concrete frame exposed on
exterior, brick spandrel walls and parapet; three-bay front × four
bays, three stories, flat roof, adjoins large factory building to rear
and connects by covered bridge to small office building. Small office
building on Harding St. is brick, four bays × three bays, two stories,
flat roof. Built c. 1920. Place of manufacture of famous racing cars
and engines in 1920s and 1930s. 5 ext. photos (1971), 1 int. photo
(1971).

Elliott's Block (later L. S. Ayres Company Warehouse Annex) (IN-60),
14–22 W. Maryland St. Brick with cast-iron, stone, and sheet-metal
trim, 72′6″ (nine-bay front), three stories, sloping roof, first-floor
openings framed by cast-iron columns, round-arched windows on
second floor and elliptical-arched windows on third floor have stone
surrounds, sheet-metal cornice. Built c. 1875. Good example of late
19th C. commercial architecture. 2 sheets (1970, including site plan,
elevation, section); 3 ext. photos (1970); 7 data pages (1970–71). NR

Harrison, Benjamin, House (IN-53), 1230 N. Delaware St. Historic
house museum of President Benjamin Harrison Foundation. Brick,
51′6″ (three-bay front) × 101′, two-and-a-half stories with basement,

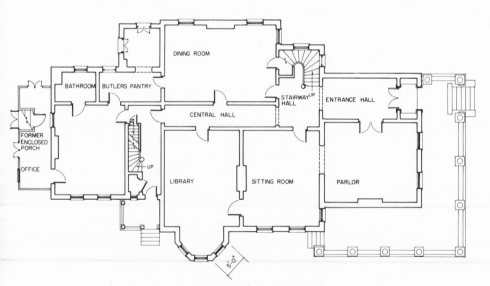

Benjamin Harrison House, first-floor plan

hipped roof, elaborate bracketed cornice, attic windows in frieze; first- and second-floor windows and main entrance have pediments on consoles; Italianate style, side hall plan. Built 1874–76; H. Brandt, architect. One-story Ionic front porch added after 1893. Restored 1974; James Associates, architects. Home of Benjamin Harrison, 23d president of the United States, from 1876 until his death 1901; houses furnishings and memorabilia of the Harrison family. 8 sheets (1970–71, including site plan, plans, elevations, section, details); 5 ext. photos (1970), 4 int. photos (1970), 2 ext. photocopies (c. 1888, n.d.); 6 data pages (1970–71). NHL NR

Historic Landmarks Foundation of Indiana. See Crown Hill Cemetery, Waiting Station (IN-56), Indianapolis.

Holler, George and Netty, House (IN-49), 324 N. Park Ave. Frame with clapboarding, 16'2" × 44', one-and-a-half stories, gable roof with gable end to street. Built c. 1863. Extensively restored 1974–75 by Historic Landmarks Foundation of Indiana; James Associates, architects. Used as Indianapolis Bicentennial headquarters, now private residence. Typical working-class house of mid-19th C. 11 sheets (1970, including site plan, plans, elevations, sections, details); 3 ext. photos (1970), 2 int. photos (1970); 9 data pages (1970–71). NR (Lockerbie Square)

"House of Twin Chimneys." See John West House (IN-36), Indianapolis.

Indiana Central State Hospital, Pathological Department Building (IN-69), 3000 W. Washington St., on hospital grounds. Museum. Brick, 68' (seven-bay front) × 72', two stories, irregular hipped roof with skylights, corbeled cornice; interior includes laboratory, study rooms, mortuary, and 160-seat auditorium. Built 1895; Adolf Scherrer, architect. Part of the state's oldest medical center and one of the most advanced for its time; facilities and equipment remain essentially unaltered; in use until 1955; under restoration as medical museum. 1 ext. photo (1970); 2 data pages (1971); HABSI form (1969). NR

Indiana National Bank (IN-62), 3 Virginia Ave., at acute-angle intersection Virginia Ave. and S. Pennsylvania St. Indiana limestone ashlar, trapezoidal shape, 100' (three-bay front) × 150' × 155' (street facades), two stories, flat roof with balustrade, paired Corinthian columns supporting carved pediment flanking entrance bay, side elevations articulated by Corinthian pilasters on rusticated podium, richly carved pediment, frieze, and spandrels, Neoclassical style, circular colored-glass skylight in two-story banking room. Built 1896–97; D. A. Bohlen & Son, architects (Oscar D. Bohlen and Hugo A. Zigrosser, designers); H. R. Saunders, sculptor. Major additions 1912, 1935, 1950, and 1958; D. A. Bohlen & Son, architects. Original building and 1912 addition demolished 1970; later multi-story additions remain. 6 ext. photos (1970), 4 int. photos (1970), 1 photocopy of site (c. 1896), 2 ext. photocopies (before 1912, c. 1915), 1 int. photocopy (1912); 9 data pages (1970–71).

Indiana Theater (IN-101), 134 W. Washington St. Concrete frame construction; exterior walls are brick on sides and rear and sheathed with white terra cotta on facade; facade has three structural bays, the outer two divided into three sub-bays each; six stories, low roof; main decorative feature of facade is great curving triangular arch with Churrigueresque framing that fills central bay above marquee; basement originally contained bowling alleys and billiard rooms; upper floors were divided between office space and theater spaces, including entrance lobby, two-and-a-half-story main lobby, and 3200-seat auditorium; elaborate plaster ornamentation fancifully based on Spanish Baroque motifs; unusual feature is large atmospheric ballroom above auditorium decorated to resemble a square surrounded by buildings, stage at one end, electric stars and projected clouds creating sky effect on elliptical domed ceiling. Major example of the great motion picture palaces of the 1920s and 1930s. Built 1927; Preston C. Rubush and Edgar G. Hunter, architects. 70'-high sign removed from W. end of facade. Basement converted to exhibition space 1958. Auditorium seating reduced to 1900 and cinerama screen installed 1960. Interior extensively remodeled to accommodate use by Indiana Repertory Theatre, 1979–80; Woollen Associates, architects. 7 ext. photos (1970), 13 int. photos (1970); 18 data pages (1970). NR

Indiana University Law School. See Maennerchor Building (IN-100), Indianapolis.

Indianapolis City Market. See Market House (IN-59), Indianapolis.

Macy, David, House, (IN-2), 408 N. Delaware St. Brick, 30'6" (three-bay front) × 62'2", two-and-a-half stories, gable roof, projecting three-sided bay on S., ornamental iron fencing, iron balcony and

Indiana Theater

David Macy House, east elevation

railing on steps, main doorway with Classical enframement, elaborate bracketed cornice with attic lights in frieze separated by wooden rosette panels, side hall plan. Built 1853 for David Macy, railroad developer; demolished. 11 sheets (1934, including site plan, plans, elevations, section, details); 1 ext. photocopy (c. 1880); 2 data pages (1934).

Maennerchor Building (Academy of Music, later Indiana University Law School) (IN-100), 102 W. Michigan St., SW. corner W. Michigan and Illinois Sts. Brick, 94' (E. front) × 150'6", three stories, red tile roofs; principal gable runs E.-W.; two slightly lower gabled wings project to S. and enclose third-floor roof deck; carved limestone trim includes doorways, window quoins, belt courses, parapet copings, and balustrades; octagonal stair tower at SE. reentrant angle, two-story concert hall on second floor with molded plaster and fresco

45

Market House (Indianapolis)

Market House (Indianapolis), interior

decorations; principal marble stair rises from marble-paneled lobby; stained-glass windows, dark wood paneling; interior and exterior have a variety of elaborate eclectic Germanic motifs. Built 1906; Swiss-born Adolf Scherrer, architect. Headquarters of the Maennerchor, a musical society founded 1854 by German immigrants; served as a cultural center for Indianapolis and a social club for the German community; major artists performed as well as a resident choir; facilities included dining hall, bar, roof garden, music library, rehearsal and meeting rooms; name changed to Academy of Music in 1918 because of anti-German sentiment. Interior altered, major rooms partitioned, and many decorative details removed 1946 when converted to Indiana University Law School; vacant after 1970; demolished 1974. 1 ext. photocopy (n.d.), 4 int. photocopies (n.d.), 10 photocopies of original drawings (c. 1906); 12 data pages (1974).

Marian College. See James A. Allison House (IN-68), Indianapolis.

Market House (now Indianapolis City Market) (IN-59), 222 E. Market St. Original portion iron frame and brick, 100' × 195', one story with raised central gabled clerestory and flat-roofed side aisles, roof supported by iron trussing, square towers flanking tall central section of main facade, brick parapets extending across front of side aisles. Built 1886; D. A. Bohlen, architect. Low flat-roofed brick additions to E. and W. 1903. Restored 1974; James Associates, architects; brick additions removed and replaced with small wings at rear connected to main building by enclosed walkway. 4 ext. photos (1970), 2 int. photos (1970), 2 ext. photocopies (c. 1888, c. 1910); 12 data pages (1971). HAER NR

Morris-Butler House (IN-52), 1204 N. Park Ave. Historic house museum of Historic Landmarks Foundation of Indiana. Red brick with stone basement, 46' (three-bay front) × 72', two-and-a-half stories with four-and-a-half-story central entrance tower, main unit and tower with slate mansard roofs, two lower rear units with gable roofs, one-story columned front porch, two-story spindle-work rear porch, Second Empire style. Built 1862 for John D. Morris; attributed to Dietrich Bohlen, architect. Restored 1964–69; James Associates, architects. Residence of the Butler family 1882–1958. 9 sheets (1970, including site plan, plans, elevations, section, details); 9 ext. photos (1970), 4 int. photos (1970); 19 data pages (1970–71); HABSI form (1969). NR

Morris-Butler House

John R. Nickum House, bedroom

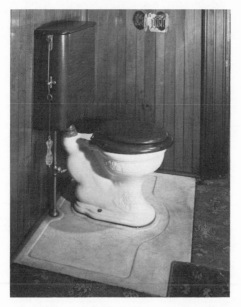

John R. Nickum House, toilet

Nickum, John R., House (James Whitcomb Riley House) (IN-51), 528 Lockerbie St. Historic house museum of James Whitcomb Riley

Memorial Association. Brick, irregular L-shaped plan, 42' (three-bay front) × 68', two-and-a-half stories, hipped roof with flat deck, projecting entrance bay, bracketed wooden cornice with attic windows in frieze, arched door and window openings with limestone trim, one-story balustraded front porch, Italianate style, original lighting and plumbing fixtures still in place, furnishings, woodwork, and interior wall finishes also preserved. Built c. 1872 for John R. Nickum. Poet James Whitcomb Riley lived in house as paying guest from 1893 until his death 1916; house has been preserved as when he lived there. 8 sheets (1970, including site plan, plans, elevations, section, details); 5 ext. photos (1970), 7 int. photos (1970), 2 ext. photocopies (one showing whole neighborhood) (c. 1901), 4 int. photocopies (c. 1900); 14 data pages (1970–71); HABSI form (1958). NHL NR

Prosser House (IN-35), 1454 E. Tenth St. Wooden frame with stucco cover, poured-concrete foundations, concrete-block studio walls, irregular cross plan, 30' × 58', one-and-a-half stories, cross-gable roof with dormers, heavy denticulated cornice, simulated corner quoining, triple-arched windows in studio, window cornices supported on consoles, elaborate plaster work on ceilings. Built 1886 by William Prosser, a plaster contractor; altered 1955 and front porch rebuilt; restored. 5 sheets (1959, including plot plan, plans, elevations, details); 3 ext. photos (1958), 3 int. photos (1958); 3 data pages (1959). NR

Riley, James Whitcomb, House. See John R. Nickum House (IN-51), Indianapolis.

"Riverdale." See James A. Allison House (IN-68), Indianapolis.

Service Supply Company, Inc. See Cole Motor Car Company Factory, Indianapolis.

Soldiers and Sailors Monument (IN-61), Monument Plaza, in the center of Monument Circle, intersection Market and Meridian Sts. Limestone-faced steel and concrete shaft, topped by observation pavilion and bronze statue of Victory, plaza diameter 342', height of monument 284', bronze collar of commemorative trophies, limestone statuary groups around base of shaft, ornamental light standards, cascade fountains to E. and W., Beaux Arts Classical design. Monument commemorates the veterans of the Mexican, Civil and Spanish-American wars; Indiana military museum in basement. Built 1888–1901; Bruno Schmitz, supervising architect; George W.

Soldiers and Sailors Monument, turn-of-century photograph

Soldiers and Sailors Monument, basement buttresses

Brewster, Nicolaus Geiger, and Rudolph Schwarz, sculptors. Site is center of original plan for the city in the circle originally reserved for the governor's residence. 8 ext. photos (1970), 3 int. photos (1970), 4 ext. photocopies (c. 1894, c. 1898, late 1920s, early 1930s); 18 data pages (1970–71). NR

Sommers, Charles B., House ("Tudor Hall") (IN-73), 3650 Cold Spring Rd. Coursed-rubble mixed with brick, rectangular with porches and porte cochere, two-and-a-half stories, basement fully exposed on W. facade, hipped roof having timbered gables with brick nogging and dormers, asphalt covering made to simulate a thick thatch, eyebrow dormers, casement windows with leaded and stained glass, rustic Jacobethan Revival style. Interior details include a room with wall covering of Rookwood Pottery tiles. Elaborate grounds originally included an artificial lake, clay tennis courts, swimming pools and bathhouse, garage and servants' quarters. Completed c. 1924; Bass Knowton and Co., architect. Charles Sommers actively participated in the designing of this uniquely personal house. House and grounds purchased c. 1957 by Tudor Hall School; classroom and dormitory buildings constructed around house, all outbuildings demolished or adapted for educational use. Complex purchased by Indianapolis Public Schools after 1970. 1 ext. photo (1970). NR

Star Service Shop (IN-72), 130 N. Illinois St. Brick, approx. 22′ × 45′, one story, gable roof with ridge perpendicular to street, parapet across facade, wide brick arch on facade visible behind recent store front. Built c. 1910, perhaps as a nickelodeon; demolished. 1 ext. photo (1970); 1 data page (1971).

Joseph W. Staub House, south elevation

Staub, Joseph W., House (IN-50), 342 N. College Ave. Brick, 24′2″ (three-bay front) × 64′3″, two stories, gable and hipped roofs, side hall plan, main entrance with molded wooden surround, cast-iron balcony on scroll brackets above door, recessed porch and projecting three-sided bay on side elevation. Built c. 1859; rear additions of early date; interior remodeled 20th C. Restored 1978–80; James Associates, architects. Example of modest house of the period. 10 sheets (1970, including plot plan, plans, elevations, section, details); 4 ext. photos (1970), 1 int. photo (1970); 10 data pages (1970–71). NR (Lockerbie Square)

"Tudor Hall." See Charles B. Sommers House (IN-73), Indianapolis.

Union Station (IN-65), 39 Jackson Pl., between Illinois and McCrea Sts. Red brick with pink granite trim, approx. 145′ square in plan with projecting bays and corner pavilions, three stories plus mezzanine and basement, picturesque roofline with large cross gable above main entrance, square corner clock tower, three-story barrel-

Union Station, interior, circular window

vaulted central waiting room with stained-glass wheel windows at each end, Romanesque Revival style. Station and adjoining iron train shed built c. 1886–88; Thomas Rodd, architect and engineer. Station remodeled 1913–14; D. A. Bohlen & Son, architects. New concourse and train shed built 1916–22; McLanahan & Bencher, architects. 8 ext. photos (1970), 5 int. photos (1970), 2 ext. photocopies (c. 1889, n.d.); 13 data pages (1971). NR

U.S. Arsenal, Arsenal Building (Arsenal Technical High School) (IN-66), 1500 E. Michigan St. Brick with limestone trim, 173' (eleven-bay front) × 63', 13' × 60' wing at rear, three stories above raised basement, hipped roof, massive three-stage projecting entrance tower with rusticated arched opening, trim of giant-order stone pilasters on one-story rusticated bases at corners of building and tower. Built 1863–65; architect undetermined; Isaac Hodgson supervised construction. Served as arsenal until 1903 when converted to educational use; became Arsenal Technical High School 1912. Interior altered and floors replaced 1932; D. A. Bohlen & Son, architects. A number of other buildings from original arsenal complex remain on 75-acre high school campus. 1 ext. photo (1970), 1 ext. photocopy (n.d.); 7 data pages (1970). NR

Vinton-Pierce House (IN-24), 1415 N. Meridian St. Brick with stone trim, 54'2" (three-bay front) × 67', two-and-a-half stories, hipped roof, stone quoining and window heads, projecting entrance pavilion, elaborate W. front doorway with Corinthian pilasters and bracketed cornice, steps flanked by lioness statues, cornice bracketed and punctuated by ovoid attic lights, Italianate style, central hall plan with cross hall, kitchen ell at rear; outbuildings included polygonal privy and brick stable. Built c. 1860; Joseph Curzon, architect. Porte cochere to N. added in 20th C. Demolished before 1970. 12 sheets (1936, including plans, elevations, details).

Webber House (IN-54), 621 Lockerbie St. Frame, L-shaped, 22' × 32', two stories, gable roof perpendicular to street, one-story rear kitchen addition, later one-story porch across front. Built c. 1873. Modest working-class house. 8 sheets (1970, including plot plan, plans, elevations, section, details); 3 data pages (1971). NR (Lockerbie Square)

West, John, House ("House of Twin Chimneys") (IN-36), 7607 Allisonville Rd. Brick, L-shaped, 33'2" (five-bay front) × 18', rear wing 25' × 32', one story, gable roofs, front block containing single room with fireplaces at each end and large exterior brick chimneys, en-

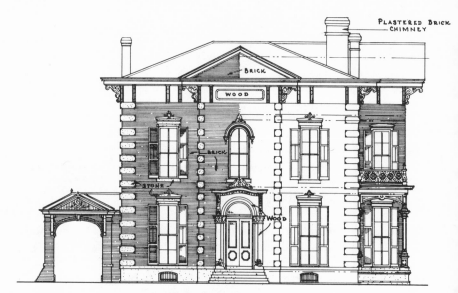

Vinton-Pierce House, west elevation

John West House, west elevation

trance doors in second and fourth bays of facade with Classical enframements, segmental arched windows. Built 1836 by John West; two rear additions containing dining room, kitchen, and bedrooms added c. 1875 and c. 1900. Among the oldest surviving houses in Marion County. 4 sheets (1959, including plans, elevations, details); 3 ext. photos (1959), 4 int. photos (1959); 3 data pages (1959).

Woodruff Place (IN-67), East, West, and Middle Drives, parallel streets bounded E. 10th St. on N., E. Michigan St. on S., Arsenal Technical High School on W., Tecumseh St. on E. Early example of residential planning in Indianapolis, platted 1872 as a "residential park," not annexed to the city until 1962; streets have center esplanades with cast-iron fountains and statuary, lots average 80' × 170'; uniform setbacks; houses are mostly frame construction, of substantial size, and date from between 1872 and c. 1920. Planner for the development was James O. Woodruff. 12 ext. photos (1970); 4 data pages (1971). NR (Woodruff Place Historic District)

Jeffersonville   **Clark County (10)**

Grisamore House (IN-18), 111–113 W. Chestnut St. Brick with stone trim, 50' (six-bay front) × 44', two-and-a-half stories on raised basement, gable roof with central pediment, double house with center party wall and paired central stairhalls; three two-story Doric

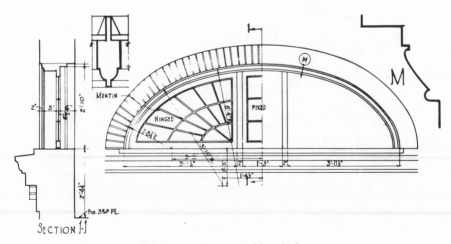

Grisamore House, gable window

columns *in antis* frame recessed entrances with elliptical lights; paired semicircular wrought-iron stairs rise 4' to entrance level; Federal and Greek Revival details. Built c. 1837 for David and Wilson Grisamore. 6 sheets (1934, including plans, elevations, details); 2 ext. photos (1934); 2 data pages (1934).

Madison   **Jefferson County (39)**

Area Study (IN-88). General study of this Ohio River town with innumerable brick buildings surviving from shortly after the platting of the town 1809 through the peak of Madison's prosperity 40 years later; includes streets, residences, gardens, the courthouse, and public, commercial, and industrial buildings; predominantly Federal and Greek Revival in style; some later building activity is represented in Victorian styles of 1860s and 1870s. 74 ext. photos (1971); 30 data pages (1971). HAER (Ben Schroeder Saddletree Factory) NR (Madison Historic District)

Area Study (Madison), iron porch detail

Area Study (Madison), wood porch detail

Bruning Carriage House (IN-122), originally 722 W. Main St., now at rear of 719 W. Main Street. Brick, 18' × 41', two stories, large double doors centered in N. facade, ornamental slate roof topped by pyramidal-roofed cupola. First floor was a single large room used to house horses, carriages, and equipment; full second-floor hayloft was reached by ladder. Built 1876–78 as outbuilding for John F. Bruning House (destroyed c. 1955), it is an unusual surviving example of post-Civil War suburban carriage houses typical in Madison. Dismantled 1978, moved to present location, adapted for commercial use. 13 data pages (1978). NR (Madison Historic District)

Christ Episcopal Church (IN-123), 506 Mulberry St. Brick, stone foundation, 56' (five-bay front) × 95', one story, steep gable roof, bell tower SW. corner, three lancet windows E. and W. ends, N. and S. facade windows separated by brick wall buttresses with stone coping, interior little altered, original glass made 1849 in Cincinnati still intact. Good example of ecclesiastical Gothic Revival. Built 1848–50; William R. West, architect. 20 data pages (1978). NR (Madison Historic District)

Colby-Jeffery House (Colby-Lanier-Jeffery House) (IN-124), 302 Elm St. Frame, approx. 42' (three-bay front) × 72' with ell to N., two-and-a-half stories on raised stone basement, gable roof. S. facade with portico with four fluted Doric columns that support a pediment forming Greek temple front, S. wall with horizontal flush board siding, entry on W. with single-story projecting Doric portico, unusual floor plan of side entry with formal rooms in main block and less formal room in ell, Greek Revival style. Built 1838–39 for Daniel Colby. J. F. D. Lanier lived here while his mansion (IN-23) was under construction. 28 data pages (1978). NR (Madison Historic District)

Commercial Buildings (IN-83), 301–315 Mulberry St. See Mulberry Street Block, Madison.

Costigan, Francis, House (IN-87), 408 W. Third St. Brick, L-shaped, 21'9" (two-bay front) × 72'2" (including c. 1890 one-story kitchen), two stories, low-pitched gable roof behind flat wooden denticulated cornice, window sills and heads, basement story and projecting porch platform of stone, wooden entry porch with two modified Corinthian columns and square pilasters supporting a flat-roofed entablature, double-light transom, side hall plan, undivided 16' × 34' double parlor with two fireplaces, semicircular front wall, ceiling

Francis Costigan House,
south elevation

Francis Costigan House,
porch with reflected ceiling
and base plans

panels with carved molding, gas fixture in central medallion. Exceptional adaptation of a row-house style in freestanding house. Built 1850–52; Francis Costigan, architect. Costigan was one of the most significant mid-19th C. architects in the Ohio River Valley. This was his last major work in Madison and his last home in the city. 6 sheets (1971, including site plan, plans, elevations, section, details); 5 ext. photos (1971), 4 int. photos (1971); 11 data pages (1971). NR (Madison Historic District)

Devenish-Haigh House (IN-125), 108 E. Third St. Brick, approx. 30′ (three-bay front) × 70′, including rear ell, two stories, gable roof with fractables above E. and W. ends, entry with transom, brick denticulated cornice, side hall plan, interior of original woodwork and built-in cupboards, late Federal style. Rear wing built 1837–39 for Soloman Devenish; sold 1852 to William Fry, who built front block in 1853; remained in Fry family until 1978. 15 data pages (1978). NR (Madison Historic District)

Eagle Cotton Mill (now Meese, Inc.) (IN-94), 108 St. Michael's Ave. Complex of industrial, Functional-style structures, main four-story loft structure approx. 75′ (six bays) × 300′ (twenty-five bays), timber post and beam framing with 24″ brick walls, stone foundation, very low gable roof, three-row segmental brick arched windows and stone sills, two-story brick NW. wing with brick smoke stack that served four boilers. Majority of structures built in 1884 by Madison firm of Robert H. Rankin and James White, builders. One-story brick office built 20th C. Cotton mill machinery removed 1932. 1 ext. photo (1971); 8 data pages (1971). NR (Madison Historic District)

East Main Street Block (IN-134), 217–229 East Main St. The buildings of the East Main Street block present a variety of typical 19th C. commercial architecture. All have been altered, but two (217–219 and 223–229 E. Main) retain much of their original character. The brick Masonic Building at 217–219, erected 1871–72, is of Second Empire style with central entry pavilion terminating in steep star-shaped roof, heavy brackets supporting a deep cornice, and mansard roof with rounded dormers; eight cast-iron engaged Corinthian columns flank shop windows and entries of this little-altered structure. The building at 223–229 E. Main is a single building constructed as four individual stores with rental space above; built in 1880–81, its Italianate design is reflected in the heavy window hoods and wide bracketed cornice; the detailed cast-iron storefront is an excellent example of typical American 19th C. commercial facades. 2 sheets (1978, elevations; 2 ext. photos (1978); 72 data pages (1978). NR (Madison Historic District)

East Main Street Row Houses (IN-133), 710–714 East Main St. Main facade rubble stone stuccoed and scored to simulate dressed stone, other facades stuccoed, rubble-stone foundation 62′ (nine-bay front) × 42′, two stories, rectangular brick additions of varying sizes to each unit, gable-roofed structure containing three units of three bays, each with identical side hall plan. Built prior to 1839. A fire mark still on the structure represents the Home Insurance Company of Lafayette, Indiana. 7 sheets (1978, including plans, elevations, section, details); 24 data pages (1978). NR (Madison Historic District)

Eckert, John, House (IN-126), 510 W. Second St. Brick main block with gable roof and frame clapboarded rear addition with shed roof, 18' (three-bay front) × 69', one story, embossed metal detailing on front molded to form corner quoins and recessed arched panels, wide cornice with console brackets, late 19th C. Italian Renaissance Revival detailing, shotgun plan. Built 1872. 3 sheets (1978, including plan, elevation, details); 7 data pages (1978). NR (Madison Historic District)

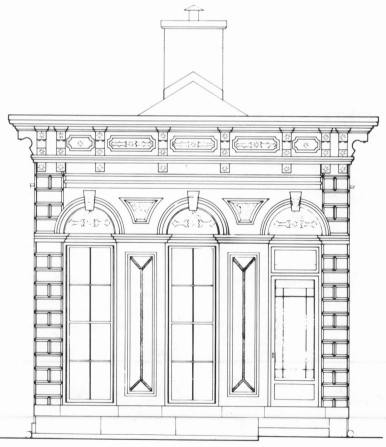

John Eckert House, south elevation

Fair Play Fire Company No. 1, south elevation

Fair Play Fire Company No. 1 (IN-90), NE. corner Main and Walnut Sts. Brick, one-and-a-half stories, gable roof with ridge perpendicular to street, 52′ three-stage corner bell and hose tower, cornices dividing stories, corners pilastered, semicircular headed windows, open wooden bell housing. Built 1850 as streetcar stable; purchased for a firehouse and tower added 1888; c. 1895 tower topped by a sheet-iron weather vane of man with a horn, "Little Jimmy," by Peter Hoffman, Madison tinsmith. Building houses oldest volunteer fire company in the state, organized 1831; company's constitution of 1841 gave it present name; located in present building since 1888. 4 ext. photos (1971); 4 data pages (1971). NR (Madison Historic District)

First Baptist Church (IN-127), 416 Vine St. Brick, rectangular with rear addition, 46' (three-bay front) × 76', two stories, gable roof on main block and pitched roof on addition, Tuscan pilasters and recessed segmental arched panels on four facades, central doorway with denticulated gable pediment supported by scrolled brackets, denticulated pediment at principal cornice, sanctuary with plaster key fretwork and egg-and-dart moldings, Greek Revival details. Built 1853–60. 4 sheets (1978, including plan, elevations, details); 10 data pages (1978). NR (Madison Historic District)

First Presbyterian Church (IN-95), 202 Broadway. Brick painted white, stone trim originally unpainted, three bays × five bays, sanctuary built to seat 600 above a windowed basement story; gable-fronted structure with broad Doric pilasters, architrave, and shallow recessed bays; entrance doors in partially projecting tower capped by copper-roofed octagonal cupola; Greek Revival style. Built 1846–47; cupola rebuilt 1868; office and Sunday school wing added to rear 1956. Church organized 1815 and divided into First and Second Presbyterian churches 1833. This is the third building of the First Presbyterian Church in Madison. 3 data pages (1971). NR (Madison Historic District)

Foster Building (IN-86), 102–106 E. Main St. Brick, 49'6" (eight-bay front) × 84' (seven bays), three stories, flat and gable roofs, bracketed decorative sheet-metal cornice; appears to be a single eight-bay building, divided into three separate buildings by party walls; cast-iron shopfronts with fluted Corinthian piers and four slender columns; windows on floors above have cast-iron sills and heads simulating carved stone. Apparently built c. 1875. Metal work probably made in Madison. Among the best of a number of cast-iron-fronted commercial buildings that line Main St. Major alterations on first floor of 106 E. Main. 3 sheets (1971, including site plan, plans, elevation, details); 8 ext. photos (1971); 4 data pages (1971). NR (Madison Historic District)

Frevert-Schnaitter House (IN-91), 740 W. Main St. Brick, approx. 45' (five-bay front) × 30' (not including rear service wing), two stories, low gable roof, brick cornice, large-scale entrance porch with two unusual octagonal columns supporting flat entablature, central hall plan, Greek Revival porch and interior woodwork, transitional Federal style. Built 1850s for August Frevert. 1 ext. photo (1971), 1 int. photo (1971); 2 data pages (1971). NR (Madison Historic District)

Historic Madison Auditorium. See Second Presbyterian Church (IN-15), Madison.

Holstein-Whitsitt House. See Jacob Shuh House (IN-92), Madison.

Hutchings, Dr. William D., Office (IN-81), 120 W. Third St. Museum owned by Historic Madison, Inc. Brick with stone lintels and sills, 18′ (two-bay front) × 34′, two stories, gable treated as pedimented front. Built c. 1830–40 as lawyer's office; occupied by Hutchings 1882–1903; waiting room and surgery on first floor, two patients' rooms above, much of Hutchings' furniture and equipment still in place. The best of several individual office buildings remaining in Madison. 5 sheets (1971, including site plan, plans, elevations, sections, details); 3 ext. photos (1971), 1 int. photo (1971); 8 data pages (1971). NR (Madison Historic District)

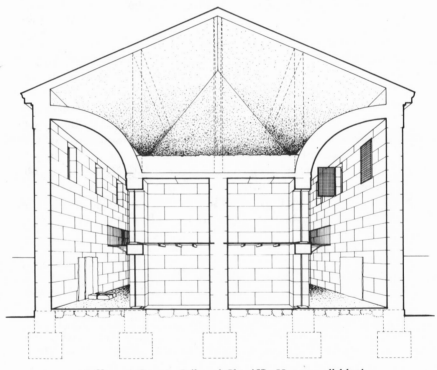

Jefferson County Jail and Sheriff's House, cell block,
perspective section

Jefferson County Jail and Sheriff's House (IN-84), Courthouse Square, SW. corner Main and Walnut Sts. Two stories, 44'4" × 88'4"; residence is brick, jail is stone, both painted; half-hipped roof covers both sections and forms broad pediment on house facade, which has a five-bay front; recessed entrance porch architecturally framed with wooden Doric pilasters and entablature; central hall plan; jail has a two-tier central cell block surrounded by peripheral passage two stories high with half-barrel vault; cell doors, locks, and window grilles of wrought iron. Built 1850; stonework and perhaps jail design by Robert McKim and James Falconer; one-story kitchen wing added 1857 (now destroyed); addition to E. and S. 1973. 10 sheets (1971, including site plan, plans, elevations, sections, details); 4 ext. photos (1971), 5 int. photos (1971); 14 data pages (1971). NR

Lanier, James F. D., House (IN-23), 500 W. First St., bounded by Elm, Vine, and First Sts., on the Ohio River. Historic house museum of the State of Indiana. Brick, 53' (three-bay front) × 64' (four bays), two-and-a-half stories, one-and-a-half-story kitchen and servants' wing to E.; low hipped roof on main block with parapet, denticulated cornice, and central anthemion; mansard roof on kitchen ell; tetrastyle Corinthian portico at S. side overlooks river; colossal-order Doric pilasters on N. facade; ornamental iron railings at both S. portico and first-floor windows on N. facade; elaborate octagonal wooden cupola crowns roof over cantilevered spiral stair; each window on N. and S. elevations is trimmed with Classical wooden pilasters and cornice; each door of main block has brick pilasters with stone bases and caps; Greek Revival style; central hall plan, two rooms each side with central cantilevered spiral stair; double parlors at W. side of central hall are separated by sliding doors with wooden Ionic columns *in antis;* marble mantels. Built 1840–44; Francis Costigan, architect. Restored 1926. James Lanier was a Madison banker who later founded a banking firm in New York City. Lanier's loans in excess of a million dollars to the State of Indiana enabled the state to equip troops during the Civil War. An Indiana State Memorial, open to the public. 15 sheets (1936, including site plan, plans, elevations, section, details); 8 ext. photos (1971), 5 int. photos (1971); HABSI form (1957). NR (Madison Historic District)

McNaughton House (IN-89), 416 E. Second St. Brick, L-shaped three-bay front, two stories, two-story and one-story service wings, gable roof, recessed entrance with Doric pilasters and entablature enframement, cast-iron balcony on scroll brackets at second floor,

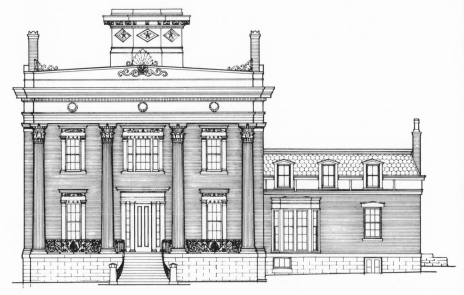

James F. D. Lanier House, south elevation

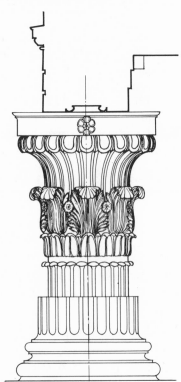

James F. D. Lanier House,
column detail

two-story gallery along ell, Greek Revival style, side hall plan, undivided double parlor, plaster ceiling panel, carved cove moldings and door frames with shells and rosettes. Rear wing probably built c. 1830s; main block built c. 1850. Front portion a superior example of the attached-house type prevalent in Madison. Adapted for commercial use. 1 ext. photo (1971), 2 int. photos (1971); 5 data pages (1971). NR (Madison Historic District)

Miller Wagon Manufacturing Shop (IN-128), 805–809 Walnut St. Brick on stone foundation, 66′ (six-bay front) × 160′, two stories with an addition, single sloping roof to W., six segmental arched windows on second floor and corresponding semicircular arched doorways on first floor composing principal facade. Originally only one-room deep with two connecting rooms on main floor and a large open space on second floor. Built 1871–72 for the wagon manufactory of Jacob Barnhardt Miller. 14 data pages (1978). NR (Madison Historic District)

Mulberry Street Block

Mulberry Street Block (IN-83), 301–315 Mulberry St. Eight adjoining rectangular brick buildings, two and three stories, gable and flat roofs, three and four bays; cornice, sills, and window moldings of pressed sheet metal and cast iron; first-floor spaces used for commercial purposes, upper levels for residences of offices. Built intermittently late 1820s to early 1840s; decorative sheet-metal and cast-iron molding added to several street-level facades, cornices, and openings 1870s. In 1850 this block had fashionable salons, restaurants, and tailors. Francis Costigan's famous hostelry, the Madison Hotel (1850), was on the adjoining block. 6 sheets (1971, including site plan, plans, details); 5 ext. photos (1971); 13 data pages (1971). NR (Madison Historic District)

Pittsburgh, Cincinnati, Chicago and St. Louis Railway Company Station (now Wilco Electric Company) (IN-93), 615 W. First St. Hard yellow brick, approx. 25' × 50', one story; hipped roof extends beyond walls to form surrounding porch supported by turned wooden posts (S. and W. sides now enclosed with concrete blocks); freight and telegraph office on W.; waiting room on E. is an octagon that rises above the main roof and has clerestory lights; Functional style, originally with Queen Anne interior details (now destroyed). Built c. 1894; discontinued as a station c. 1930; altered for business use. 1 ext. photo (1971); 4 data pages (1971). NR (Madison Historic District)

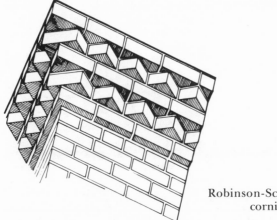

Robinson-Schofield House,
cornice detail

Robinson-Schofield House (IN-82), 221 W. Second St. Museum. Brick, L-shaped, 32'4" (four-bay front) × 58', two stories on high basement, half-hipped roof, gable on ell, round brick relieving arches above first-floor windows on main facade, segmental brick arches above other windows, one-story frame shed at rear, Federal style. Probably built by William Robinson for Alexander Lanier. It is traditionally held that the Grand Lodge Free and Accepted Masons of Indiana was organized in the house January 12, 1818. Restored by Masonic Heritage Foundation. 8 sheets (1971, including site plan, plans, elevations, section, details); 3 ext. photos (1971); 11 data pages (1971). NR (Madison Historic District)

Saint Michael's Catholic Church (IN-129), 519 E. Third St. Coursed-ashlar limestone with larger stones at corners forming quoins, 54′ (three-bay front) × 124′ (seven bays), simple gable structure with exterior adornment limited to simple carved stone window and door-hood moldings, a small stone shield with crosslet and a large carved stone roundel on principal facade, three-story bell tower at NW. corner, simple but much-altered interior with original ogee-vaulted ceiling, Gothic Revival style. Built 1838–39; oldest church building in Madison. Traditionally believed to be constructed of stone from the Madison and Indianapolis Railroad rock cut at the west edge of Madison. (see HAER IN-19). 26 data pages (1978). NR (Madison Historic District)

Saint Michael's Rectory (IN-85), 519 E. Third St., at NW. corner Saint Michael's Church. Stuccoed rubble stone with brick cornice, 34′2″ (three irregularly spaced bays) × 32′2″ (four bays), two stories on sloping site with basement fully exposed on S., hipped roof, modified central hall plan. Built c. 1860 as priests' living quarters and offices. Forms complete church group with adjacent stone sanctuary and tower of Saint Michael's. 7 sheets (1971, including site plan, plans, elevations, section, details); 5 ext. photos (1971), 1 int. photo (1971); 12 data pages (1971). NR (Madison Historic District)

Saint Michael's Rectory, south elevation

71

Sanders-McNaughton House. See McNaughton House (IN-89), Madison.

Second Presbyterian Church (now Historic Madison Auditorium) (IN-15), NE. corner West and Third Sts. Stuccoed brick, approx. 70' (seven-bay front) × 50', one story on raised basement, low gable roof, pseudo-octastyle temple front with six Doric pilasters flanking two fluted Doric columns *in antis,* Greek Revival style, segmental vaulted paneled ceiling supported by lattice wooden trusses at approx. 16' on center. Built 1834; Edwin J. Peck, architect. Interior altered 1928. 8 sheets (1934, including plans, elevations, sections, details); 4 ext. photos (1934, 1971); 1 data page (1934). NR (Madison Historic District)

Shrewsbury, Charles L., House (IN-8), 301 W. First St. Private historic house museum. Brick, 48'10" (three-bay front) × 42'7", two-and-a-half stories, low hipped roof with flat deck (balustrade now removed), one-and-a-half-story servants' wing and one-story kitchen at W.; each corner of main block has brick pilasters with stone caps; wide bead and reel cornice; attic windows in frieze; recessed entry at N. elevation has stone-eared pedimental frame and stone steps; porch at S. elevation has two lotus-bud columns and stone steps down to garden; first-floor windows on N. and S. elevations have

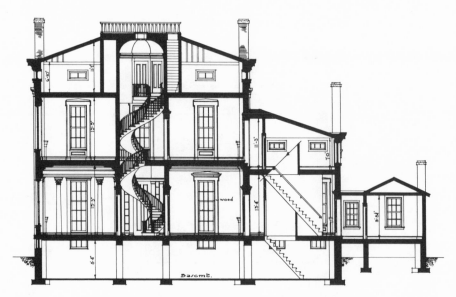

Charles L. Shrewsbury House, longitudinal section

iron balconies; central hall plan with freestanding and self-supporting spiral stairway, domed stairwell; paired Corinthian columns separate double parlors; Greek Revival style. Built 1846 for Capt. Charles Lewis Shrewsbury; Francis Costigan, architect. Restored. 16 sheets (1934, including plans, elevations, sections, details); 8 ext. photos (1934, 1971, n.d.), 8 int. photos (1971, n.d.); 2 data pages (1934); HABSI form (1958). NR (Madison Historic District)

Shuh, Jacob, House (IN-92), 718 W. Main St. Brick, five-bay front, two stories on low basement, two-story rear service wing, low hipped roof once crowned by widow's walk, denticulated cornice, bead and reel moldings on entablature and recessed entrance; door enframement of Doric pilasters, entablature, and sidelights; brick pilasters with Doric caps at all four corners; central hall plan; central stair rises three flights to attic; undivided double parlor with ogee-arched wooden mantels and finely detailed large-scale treatment of ceilings bordered in recessive carved bands of molding. Probably built in 1840s; attributed to Francis Costigan, architect. Unusual in Madison, it stands in a class just below the Lanier and Shrewsbury mansions. 1 ext. photo (1971), 1 int. photo (1971); 2 data pages (1971). NR (Madison Historic District)

Sullivan, Jeremiah, House (IN-9), 304 W. Second St. Historic house museum owned by Historic Madison, Inc. Brick, L-shaped, 30'2" (three-bay front) × 75'4", main block two-and-a-half stories on raised basement, ell two stories with two-story gallery on E., gable roofs, main (S.) doorway with elliptical fanlight and sidelights flanked by colonettes and outlined with beading, approached by stone steps with iron railing, side hall plan, basement kitchen, Federal style. Built 1818 for Jeremiah Sullivan. 10 sheets (1934, including plans, elevations, section, details); 10 ext. photos (1934, 1971, n.d.), 5 int. photos (1971); 1 data page (1934). NR (Madison Historic District)

Talbott, Richard, House (IN-130), 301 W. Second St. Brick, L-shaped, 30' (five-bay front) × 40' with rear wing (30' × 48'), two stories on raised basement, gable roof with end chimneys, central doorway with projecting denticulated cornice and consoles, central hall plan, early 19th C. Classical interior details, Federal style. Built 1819–20. 6 sheets (1978, including site plan, plans, elevations, section, details); 10 data pages (1978). NR (Madison Historic District)

Walnut Street Fire Company No. 4 (IN-131), 808 Walnut St. Brick, 27′ (three-bay front) × 75′, two stories, broken-pediment facade; pressed-tin cornice, brackets, window hoods; occulus window in gable; Italianate style. Built 1874, probably to the designs of Madison architect Alexander White. Cast-iron streetfront added 1894; original bell cupola removed 1933. 20 data pages (1978). NR (Madison Historic District)

Washington Fire Company No. 2 (IN-132), 104 W. Third St. Brick, 27′ (three-bay front) × 80′ (five bays), two stories, hose and bell tower on W. side; originally first story of main facade had center arched fire engine bay with flanking doors, replaced by overhead door in 1964; narrow cornice; pedimented main facade; gable roof; second-floor meeting hall with elaborate interior woodwork, including molded plaster floral ceiling panels and a screen formed by two Corinthian columns and two engaged pilasters; Greek Revival style. Built 1848–49; designed by Matthew Temperly and William or Isaac Sutton. Washington Fire Engine Company No. 2, organized 1846, is still a volunteer fire department; the building is thought to be the oldest firehouse still in use in the state. 20 data pages (1978). NR (Madison Historic District)

West Main Street Block (IN-135), 201–215 W. Main St. These six brick structures, all built c. 1825–40, have been altered and now represent an assortment of late 19th C. commercial styles. Most are ornamented with locally produced metal cornices and window caps that cover earlier building fabric. A chamfered corner entrance with single iron supporting column is found at each end of the block. 2 sheets (1978); 73 data pages (1978). NR (Madison Historic District)

Wilco Electric Company. See Pittsburgh, Cincinnati, Chicago & St. Louis Railway Company Station (IN-93), Madison.

Madison Vicinity   **Jefferson County (39)**

Bachman House (IN-121), Lonesome Hollow, 0.4 mi. S. of Telegraph Rd. Stone, rectangular, dogtrot plan, 51′ (SW. front) × 20′, two stories, gable roof, exterior end chimneys, central breezeway. Built c. 1825–50. 7 sheets (1978, including site plan, plans, elevations, section, details); 8 data pages (1978). NR (Madison Historic District)

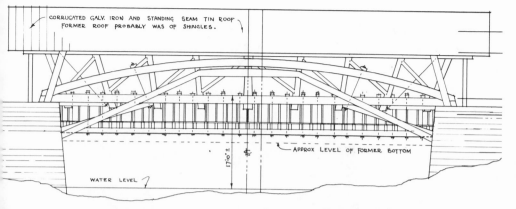

Whitewater Canal Aqueduct, north elevation

Metamora   Franklin County (24)

Whitewater Canal Aqueduct (IN-20), spanning Duck Creek, 200' S. of
U.S. Rt. 52, 0.5 mi. E. of Metamora. Part of Whitewater Canal State
Monument. Heavy wooden bow truss, span approx. 80', width
approx. 16', gable roof. Built c. 1843; rebuilt 1847 after flood; extra
triangulation bracing members added later to each of the two
trusses; strengthened structurally 1868 and 1901; reconstructed
1948–49, with Burr trusses and a few other original timbers reused.
Part of Whitewater Canal system linking Cincinnati, Ohio, and
Hagerstown, Indiana. 4 sheets (1934, including plans, elevations,
sections, framing details); 2 ext. photos (1934), 2 structural detail
photos (1934); 1 data page (1934). NR (Whitewater Canal Historic
District)

Michigan City   La Porte County (46)

Michigan City Lighthouse (IN-99), in Washington Park, adjacent to
Michigan City Harbor. Old Lighthouse Museum, Michigan City Historical Society. Brick, 50' (three-bay front) × 30', two-and-a-half
stories, sloping site with basement exposed on S., gable roof, Palladian windows on E. front, second story sheathed with wooden shingles, gabled wall dormer above main entrance, one-story columnar
porches centered on E. and W., porch on E. semi-elliptical with
balustraded deck, modified central hall plan. Built 1857–58, with
1858 worked in brick on S. side; major addition to N. side 1904–05,

Michigan City Lighthouse, south elevation

nearly doubling floor space, fenestration changed, shingles and porches added, and lighthouse cupola removed. Restored 1971 to appearance after 1904 alterations. Until 1934 served as navigational lighthouse for shipping along S. shore of Lake Michigan; staffed by a female lightkeeper, Harriet Colfax, for over 40 years. 9 sheets (1971, including site plan, plans, elevations, section, details); 5 data pages (1971). NR

Milton Vicinity   **Wayne County (89)**

"Beechwood." See Kinsey, Isaac, House and Farm (IN-109), Milton Vicinity.

Daniels House (IN-117), W. side State Rt. 1, 3.5 mi. S. of Milton. Frame with clapboarding, L-shaped, five-bay front, two stories with one-and-a-half-story ell, gable roofs, arcaded one-story entrance porch; Greek Revival details include heavy cornice with wide frieze,

76

short cornice returns on gable ends, pilaster strips at corners; central hall plan; walnut woodwork; built-in cabinets (one a secretary) flanking mantels in two front parlors; excellently preserved graining and marbling in stairhall and upstairs rooms. Probably built 1850s. Typical mid-19th C. farmhouse of the area. 9 ext. photos (1975), 6 int. photos (1975).

Daniels House

Kinsey, Isaac, House and Farm ("Beechwood") (IN-109), 502 E. Sarver Rd., 0.25 mi. S. of Lindsey Rd. Brick, L-shaped with three projecting bays, 80′ (nine-bay front) × 53′, two-and-a-half stories, hipped slate roof with square cupola, E. and W. bays having octagonal roofs with sheet-metal finials, two-story cast-iron porch, sheet-metal cornice, modified central hall plan, conservatory, original mantels (some marble) and woodwork, unusual heating and water-heating systems, Bracketed Italianate style. Built 1871; J. Stover, Richmond, Indiana, architect. First owner Isaac Kinsey, farmer and industrialist. Very large and well-preserved example of Italianate farmhouse with 8 of

77

Isaac Kinsey House

original 14 outbuildings remaining. 9 sheets (1974, including site
plan, plans, elevations); 12 ext. photos (1975), 9 int. photos (1975), 4
ext. photocopies (n.d.), 1 photocopy of farm plan (c. 1890), 1 photocopy of plaque naming builder and artisans; 15 data pages (1974).
NR

100 Block of North Main Street (IN-136), 100 block of N. Main St. Buildings constructed from 1880s to early 1900s after fire 1872 destroyed most of downtown commercial district; many alterations c. 1920–30; demolished 1977. Mishawaka, formed in 1838, was a prosperous industrial town benefiting from proximity to bog iron deposits and from its location by the rapids of the St. Joseph River. 9 ext. photos (1977). See entries below (IN-137–144) for additional photos of individual buildings.

100 Block of North Main Street, Mishawaka Trust and Savings Company (IN-137), NW. corner Main St. and Lincolnway West. Limestone with concrete, two stories, five-bay front, flat roof with parapet, entablature composed of cornice and frieze with carved name of building, bays punctuated by pilasters, recessed main entrance framed by Ionic columns and small entablature, Classical details; interior divided into shops on first floor, office space on second. Built 1918; exterior signs and storefront fixtures added, interior space partitioned, drop ceilings installed on first floor, n.d.; demolished 1977. 10 ext. photos (1977), 17 int. photos (1977). See 100 Block of North Main Street (IN-136) for additional photos.

100 Block of North Main Street (IN-138), 107–109 N. Main St. Wooden frame with brick cladding, cast-iron trim, two stories, six-bay front, flat roof, denticulated cornice on 107, sheet-metal cap on 109, stories divided by projecting cast-iron cornice, cast-iron column at mid-point of lower facade, two shops in two major bays. Built c. 1880; extensively remodeled, including addition of modern storefronts and modern windows on second floor, cornice possibly once extended across entire facade, interior remodeled, n.d.; demolished 1977. 4 ext. photos (1977), 2 int. photos (1977). See 100 Block of North Main Street (IN-136) for additional photos.

100 Block of North Main Street, Kamm Building (IN-139), 111 N. Main St. Wooden frame with sandstone cladding, cast-iron trim, three stories, two-bay front, flat roof with parapet, entablature with denticulated cornice, Ionic pilasters dividing bays, two groups of two windows, arched openings on third story, rectangular windows with transoms on second story, second and third stories divided by carved stone spandrels, shop on first floor, office spaces on remaining floors, pressed-tin roof and mosaic floor on first level. Built c. 1880; modern storefront added, interior remodeled, n.d.; demolished

1977. 4 ext. photos (1977), 8 int. photos (1977). See 100 Block of North Main Street (IN-136) for additional photos.

100 Block of North Main Street (IN-140), 113 N. Main St. Wooden frame, stone with limestone trim, two stories, three-bay front, flat roof, cornice, arched windows with limestone arch and keystone, cast-iron lintels, shop on first floor. Built c. 1900; modern storefront added, interior remodeled, n.d.; demolished 1977. 3 ext. photos (1977), 1 int. photo (1977). See 100 Block of North Main Street (IN-136) for additional photos.

100 Block of North Main Street (IN-141), 115 N. Main St. Wooden frame, brick with cast-iron and stone trim, two stories, three-bay front, flat roof, elaborate cornice of corbeled brick, arched openings on second floor with stone keystones, cast-iron sills, shop on first floor. Built c. 1880; modern storefront added, modern windows installed on second floor, remainder of window arch bricked in, interior remodeled, n.d.; demolished 1977. 3 ext. photos (1977), 1 int. photo (1977). See 100 Block of North Main Street (IN-136) for additional photos.

100 Block of North Main Street (IN-142), 117–119 N. Main St. Wooden frame, brick with cast-iron trim, two stories, five-bay front, corbeled flat roof, brick cornice with raised segmental arch over center bay, arched openings on second floor with cast-iron surrounds and sills, two shops in two major bays. Built c. 1880; modern storefronts added, interior altered, n.d.; demolished 1977. 3 ext. photos (1977), 2 int. photos (1977). See 100 Block of North Main Street (IN-136) for additional photos.

100 Block of North Main Street (IN-143), 121–125 N. Main St. Wooden frame with stuccoed brick, brick siding, sheet-metal trim, ten-bay front, four-story central section flanked by three-story sections, flat roof with parapet, cornice; three arched bays flanked by pilasters on S. section; central section has large arch over three bays with single bay to S., circular motif with K in middle above single bay; N. section similar to S. section; three shops in three major bays. Built 1892; modern storefronts added, interior altered, n.d.; northern section altered, stuccoed over, changed into four bays divided by piers, interior floor heights altered to accommodate four floors, 1937; demolished 1977. 9 ext. photos (1977), 3 int. photos (1977). See 100 Block of North Main Street (IN-136) for additional photos.

100 Block of North Main Street (IN-144), 111 W. First St. Wooden frame with brick siding, one story, four-bay front, flat roof with parapet, bracketed cornice, large showroom windows, recessed main entrance, showroom with pressed-tin ceiling. Date of construction not determined; demolished 1977. 5 ext. photos (1977), 3 int. photos (1977). See 100 Block of North Main Street (IN-136) for additional photos.

Mitchell   Lawrence County (47)

Riley School (IN-147), 7th and College Sts. Brick with limestone trim, two stories on raised basement, five-bay front, hipped roof, main entrance through rusticated limestone arch, rusticated limestone arched windows above entrance with inscribed panel, limestone lintels on basement windows, limestone belt course between basement and first story, flat-topped brick segmental arches on first-story windows, round brick arches on second-story windows, Richardsonian Romanesque details, cruciform plan. Built 1903; addition of fire escape, n.d.; demolished 1977. Served as elementary and high school for over 70 years; astronaut Virgil "Gus" Grissom among alumni. 3 ext. photos (1977), 3 int. photos (1977).

Mongo   La Grange County (44)

O'Ferrell, John, Store (IN-148), NE. corner West and Second Sts. Frame with clapboarding, 25' (three-bay front) × 46' (four bays), two stories with one-story additions at S., N., and E.; two sets of double doors and two windows are separated by five Doric pilasters on first floor of main facade; shed-roof porch is later addition; second story and gable end form temple front with eliptical window motif in gable; Greek Revival style. Built 1832 by John O'Ferrell. 4 sheets (1975, including plans, elevations); 5 data pages (1975). NR

Morris Vicinity   Ripley County (69)

Nobbe, Marie K., House (IN-149), corner Center Rd. and State Rt. 46, approx. 1 mi. E. of Morris. Brick on raised stone foundation, 44' (five-bay front) × 32' (four bays) with a 26' × 32' rear ell, two-and-a-half stories with gable roof and paired chimneys at gable ends, shaped-stone lintels and sills with large six-over-six windows; narrow cornice with brackets has gable return; center recessed entry with transom, small wooden Greek Revival portico; center hall plan with four rooms on both first and second floors; late Greek Revival with some early Italianate details. The house originally had outbuildings, including a brick summer kitchen and a gazebo. 8 sheets (n.d., including site plan, plans, elevations, section).

Mount Auburn   Wayne County (89)

Huddleston House (IN-110), S. side of Main St., U.S. Rt. 40, approx. 250′ E. of intersection with East St. Museum. Brick, L-shaped, 50′3″ (six-bay front) × 44′5″ (including ell), sloping site with three stories exposed in front and two stories in rear, gable roofs; main block has three rooms per floor, arranged linearly, simple wooden interior trim, one-story porch on S. Surviving outbuildings include two barns, a smokehouse, and a springhouse. Probably built 1839–40 for John Huddleston; remained in Huddleston family until 1934. Served as an inn on the National Road (U.S. Rt. 40) when the road was an important westward migration route. Restored by Historic Landmarks Foundation of Indiana as a regional office and museum. 8 sheets (1974, including site plan, plans, elevations); 7 ext. photos (1975), 5 int. photos (1975); 8 data pages (1974); HABSI form (1962). NR

Huddleston House

Administration Building, Ball State University (IN-150), University Ave., W. of McKinley Ave., on Ball State campus. Brick with stone trim; three-bay main block with nine-bay balancing wings organized as three bays, each separated by engaged pilasters; three stories on a raised basement; gable roof of main block forms pediment of third-story portico; Neoclassical style. Built 1899 for use as classroom, studios, and university president's apartment. 9 sheets (n.d., including plans, elevations).

Garner, Job, House (IN-154), NW. corner County Rds. 700W and 400N (Bethel Pike). Frame, 31' (three-bay front) × 31' (three bays) with frame and brick additions to W. and N., two stories on raised foundation, hipped roof, door with sidelights and transom, center hall plan; interior woodwork, mantels, and built-in cupboards show Greek Revival influence. 6 sheets (n.d., including site plan, plans, elevations).

Smith, Isaac, House (IN-151), 513 E. Main St. Brick, L-shaped, 60'5" (three-bay front with double windows) × 40'10", two-and-a-half stories, two-story ell with a two-story gallery on E. side; main block has gable roof with corbeled brick frieze and wooden modillion cornice, a pair of chimneys at each end; doorway has Doric pilasters with scroll-bracket entablature, recessed entry with three-part transom and sidelights; main block has center hall plan with two rooms on each side. Built c. 1847 by Isaac P. Smith, master builder and contractor, who built the house for himself. 9 sheets (n.d., including site plan, plans, elevations, section, details); 7 data pages (1975).

Roberts, Gaines Hardy, House ("Old Stone House") (IN-13), State Rt. 662, 1.4 mi. E. of Newburgh. Sandstone, 50'4" (five-bay front) × 32' (three bays), two stories, one-story addition to NE., gable roof,

Gaines Hardy Roberts House, south elevation

Brown-Augustine House, north elevation

dressed-stone facade with other walls of rubble, round-arched main doorway with fanlight, four exterior end chimneys, central hall plan. Built c. 1835 for Gaines Hardy Roberts; John Meinhardt, contractor. Kitchen addition 1931; two-story portico at S. after 1935. 8 sheets (1933–34, including plans, elevations, details); 1 ext. photo (1933); 3 data pages (1933–34); HABSI form (1958). NR

New Carlisle Vicinity   La Porte County (46)

Brown-Augustine House (IN-21), U.S. Rt. 20, 3 mi. W. of New Carlisle. Frame with clapboarding, T-shaped, 50′3″ (seven-bay front) × 31′, formal temple-with-wings plan, central two-story block with four-column portico, symmetrical one-story one-room wings, simple gable roofs, Greek Revival style. Built c. 1834 by Henry Brown. Kitchen addition at SE. Burned c. 1950. 10 sheets (1936, including plans, elevations, section, details).

New Harmony   Posey County (65)

1830 Owen House. See Vondegrift House (IN-33), New Harmony.

Opera House. See Rappite Community House No. 4 (IN-32), New Harmony.

Owen, David Dale, House (IN-4), N. side Church St., between Main and West Sts. Brick 57′2″ × 69′4″, one-and-a-half stories, picturesquely shaped roof with ornamental chimney caps and pagoda-roofed cupola, conical tower above round room, exotic fenestration patterns including round-, triangular-, and flat-headed windows, two oriel windows on S. facade, elaborate metal work including cast-iron window hoods, roof crestings, and framing of porches at S. and W., Gothic Revival details. Built 1859 as a laboratory by Dr. Owen, a pioneer U.S. geologist and son of Robert Owen, founder of the utopian Owenite Community. 8 sheets (1934, including plans, elevations, details); 4 ext. photos (1934, 1940); 2 data pages (1934). NHL NR (New Harmony Historic District)

Poet's House. See Rappite House (IN-37), New Harmony.

Rapp-Maclure-Owen House (IN-161), NW. corner Church and Main Sts. Brick, L-shaped, 82′4″ × 75′2″, one story on a raised stone

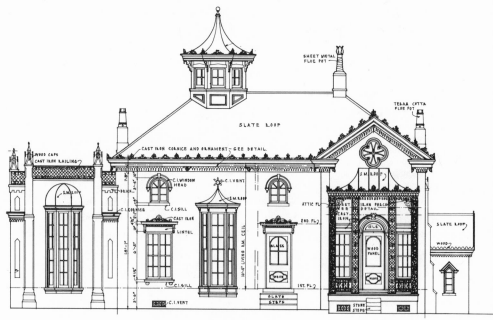

David Dale Owen House, south elevation

basement, large twelve-over-twelve windows with exterior sills of black walnut, flat-roofed porches with Doric columns and wide cornice on W., S., and E., later addition on N. and W. elevations, elaborate interior woodwork, Greek Revival style. Built 1844 by Alexander Maclure on the foundation of George Rapp's 1816 mansion, which had been destroyed by fire. Occupied 1850–60 by David Dale Owen. 10 data pages (1959). NHL NR (New Harmony Historic District)

Rappite Community House No. 2 (IN-5), 410 N. Main St., between Granary and Church Sts. Museum, part of New Harmony State Memorial. Brick, 82' (six-bay front) × 45' (three bays), two-and-a-half stories, unusual hipped gambrel roof with dormers, 1821 Rappite sundial on S. wall. Built 1816 for George Rapp as dormitory for unmarried men; purchased 1824 by Robert Owen for the Owenite Community; altered internally after 1830 to accommodate store and residence; later porch on W. elevation removed 1950s. While owned by Owenite Community, building housed first Pestalozzian school in America. Now owned by Indiana Department of Natural Resources. 9 sheets (1934, including plans, elevations, details); 3 ext. photos

(1934, 1940, 1958), 1 int. photo (1958), 1 ext. photocopy (1907); 2 data pages (1934). NHL NR (New Harmony Historic District)

Rappite Community House No. 2 Annex (Rappite Dye House) (IN-38), SE. corner Main and Granary Sts. Brick, 22′ × 29′ (original section) plus 17′ × 22′ brick extension, two stories, gable roof, working areas on first floor, living areas above. Built c. 1816; one-story log addition after 1824; converted late 19th C. to a residence; restored 1958. Originally used as a dormitory and later as a dye house by the Harmony Society, later by the Owenite Community. 4 sheets (1958, including plans, elevations, section, details); 2 ext. photos (1958), 3 int. photos (1958); 3 data pages (1958). NHL NR (New Harmony Historic District)

Rappite Community House No. 3 (Rappite Tavern) (IN-39), S. side Church St., between Main and Brewery Sts. Brick, 46′ (three-bay front) × 76′, three stories, nearly flat roof, sheet-metal bracketed cornice and window head trim dating from 1890. Built 1823 as a dormitory; converted to a tavern 1826; rebuilt 1890; demolished 1960s. Originally owned by the Harmony Society, later by the Owenite Community. Served as Robert Owen's headquarters. 3 sheets (1958, including plans, elevations); 2 ext. photos (1958, 1959); 3 data pages (1958).

Rappite Community House No. 4 (now Opera House) (IN-32), N. side Church St., between Brewery and East Sts. Museum, part of New Harmony State Memorial. Brick, two stories, gable roof perpendicular to street. Built 1823 as large communal residence; remodeled late 19th C. into theater-opera house with facade of two-story central pedimented entrance bay flanked by two bays with arcuated fenestration and corbeled brick cornices; converted 1914 to a garage; restored 1968 as a theater. Originally owned by the Harmony Society, later by the Owenite Community. Now owned by Indiana Department of Natural Resources. 5 ext. photos (1940), 1 ext. photocopy (before remodeling). NHL NR (New Harmony Historic District)

Rappite Dye House. See Rappite Community House No. 2 Annex (IN-38), New Harmony.

Rappite Fort. See Rappite Granary (IN-31), New Harmony.

Rappite Granary (Rappite Fort) (IN-31), S. side Granary St., between Main and West Sts. Coursed-rubble sandstone with brick on upper

Rappite Community House No. 4

portion of gable end, two-and-a-half stories, gable roof, open plan, narrow vertical vent slots. Built c. 1815. Served as community storage facility for the Rappites, also used as factory, and designed to provide protection if needed. 1 ext. photo (1940). NHL NR (New Harmony Historic District)

Rappite House (Poet's House) (IN-37), NE. corner Granary and West Sts. Frame with clapboarding, two-story section 20' × 29', one-story kitchen wing 16' × 11', gable roofs, side entrance, typical Rappite plan and construction, living room and kitchen on first floor, bedrooms above. Built 1815; wing added 1827; restored c. 1957. Originally owned by the Harmony Society, later by the Owenite Community. 5 sheets (1958, 1959, including plans, elevations, section, details); 2 ext. photos (1958), 3 int. photos (1958); 3 data pages (1958). NHL NR (New Harmony Historic District)

Rappite House (Rawlings House) (IN-43), N. side Granary St., between West and Main Sts. Frame with clapboarding, two stories with one-story ell, gable roof. Built 1815; restored. Originally owned by the Harmony Society, later by the Owenite Community. 1 ext. photo

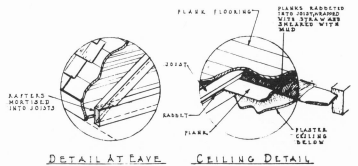

DETAIL AT EAVE   CEILING DETAIL

Rappite House (Poet's House), structural details, "Dutch biscuit" insulation

(1958), 3 int. photos (1958); 1 data page (1961). NHL NR (New Harmony Historic District)

Rappite House (Salomon Wolf House) (IN-22), originally N. side South St., between Main and Brewery Sts., moved 1975 to SE. corner Brewery and Granary Sts. Museum. Brick, two stories, gable roof, side entrance on narrow E. gable end. Built c. 1823; renovated 1970. Typical of small Rappite dwellings. Now owned by Historic New Harmony, Inc. 1 ext. photo (1940). NHL NR (New Harmony Historic District)

Rappite Tavern. See Rappite Community House No. 3 (IN-39), New Harmony.

Rawlings House. See Rappite House (IN-43), New Harmony.

Schnee House (IN-30), Tavern St., between Main and Brewery Sts. Frame with unpainted clapboarding, two-and-a-half stories, gable roof, side entrance, typical Rappite frame construction and mud-and-straw "Dutch biscuit" insulation. Built 1815; demolished 1940. 3 photos of construction details (1940), 1 ext. photocopy (c. 1903).

Vondegrift House (1830 Owen House) (IN-33), 529 Tavern St., at Brewery St. Museum. Brick, five-bay front, two stories, hipped roof, one-story brick wing at W. with gable roof parallel to street. Built by Rappite Community; wing destroyed prior to 1970, rebuilt 1979. Now owned by Historic New Harmony, Inc. 3 ext. photos (1940). NHL NR (New Harmony Historic District)

Wolf House. See Rappite House (IN-22), New Harmony.

Noblesville Vicinity   Hamilton County (29)

Conner Prairie Pioneer Settlement (IN-40), W. side Allisonville Rd., 4 mi. S. of Noblesville. Private museum operated by Earlham College. A group of restored and reconstructed buildings on the site of the early 19th C. William Conner farm. Conner's 1823 house is surrounded by workshops, homes, and outbuildings moved from other Indiana sites and used in this outdoor historical museum to interpret the life of central Indiana settlers of 1836. 1 photocopy of sketch plan of farm (c. 1937–38); 4 data pages (1961).

Conner Prairie Pioneer Settlement, William Conner House (IN-46), W. side Allisonville Rd., 4 mi. S. of Noblesville. Museum. Brick (Flemish bond on W. facade), five-bay front, two-story main section, one-and-a-half-story rear kitchen ell with beehive oven, gable roofs, central hall plan with two rooms on each floor. Interior woodwork elaborate for wilderness home; each of the four principal rooms have carved mantels and four-door cupboards flanking fireplaces. Conner is thought to have employed a woodcarver from the East who lived in the house until woodwork was completed. Built 1823; restored 1937 when porch and columns were added to front of house. First brick house in "New Purchase" of Indiana. 3 ext. photos (c. 1937–38), 1 int. photo (c. 1937–38); HABSI form (1960). NR

Conner Prairie Pioneer Settlement, Loom House (IN-47), W. side Allisonville Rd., 4 mi. S. of Noblesville. Museum. Three-bay front × two bays, one story, gable roof, conventional stud-wall construction with exterior finish in rough-sawn board and batten, single room, unusual wide-plank flooring with dovetailed joints. Built early 19th C.; moved to present site and restored 1937. 1 int. photo (c. 1937–38).

Conner Prairie Pioneer Settlement, Still House (IN-45), W. side Allisonville Rd., 4 mi. S. of Noblesville. Museum. Log, three-bay front × one bay, one story, gable roof, porch with cantilevered shed roof. Built early 19th C.; moved from Brown County and restored 1937. 1 ext. photo (c. 1937–38).

Conner Prairie Pioneer Settlement, Trading Post (Nichols Homestead) (IN-44), W. side Allisonville Rd., 4 mi. S. of Noblesville. Museum. Log, three-bay facade, one story, gable roof continued over front porch, exterior stone chimney. Built 1801; moved from Brown County and restored 1937. 1 ext. photo (c. 1937–38), 2 int. photos (c. 1937–38).

Conner Prairie Pioneer Settlement, Doan House (IN-96), W. side Allisonville Rd., 4 mi. S. of Noblesville. Frame with clapboarding, L-shaped, 30'4" (five-bay front) × 44'9" (including rear ell), two stories, gable roofs, doors in second and fourth bays of facade, simple wooden trim. Traditional building date 1833; numerous interior changes; owned by Doan family 1856–1972; served as inn for many years; restored as inn. Original location unknown; moved to Westfield, Hamilton County, probably 1850s; moved to Conner Prairie Pioneer Settlement 1972. 3 sheets (1974, including plans, elevations, isometric of framing); 5 ext. photos (1975), 6 int. photos (1975); 7 data pages (1974).

Nichols Homestead. See Conner Prairie Pioneer Settlement, Trading Post (IN-44), Noblesville Vicinity.

North Manchester   Wabash County (85)

North Manchester Public Library (IN-152), Main St. Brick on dressed-stone foundation; 55'1¼" (five-bay front) × 37', two stories, gable roof with fractable, projecting two-story entry pavilion with battered base at W. end main facade, segmental rowlock arches on first floor S. facade; stained glass, interior woodwork, and surviving original furnishings show strong Arts and Crafts influence. Built 1911; Patton & Miller, Chicago, architects. Unique among Carnegie libraries in the Midwest because of its ecclectic style with medieval overtones. 6 sheets (1975, including site plan, plans, elevations).

Paoli   Orange County (59)

Orange County Courthouse (IN-29), intersection State Rts. 37 and 156. Brick with stone trim, five bays × five bays, two stories on sloping site, basement exposed on S., gable roof with simple domed clock tower, monumental Doric hexastyle portico on S. supporting continuous entablature, Doric pilasters on rear and side elevations; two

North Manchester Public Library, south elevation

Orange County Courthouse

double iron stairways from ground to first floor and under portico from first floor to second-floor courtroom, Greek Revival style. Built 1847–50; interior severely altered 20th C. 4 ext. photos (1940); HABSI form (1970). NR

Pendleton Vicinity   **Madison County (48)**

Fussell, Samuel, Log House (IN-153), S. side State Rt. 38, 3 mi. E. of Pendleton. Log, 26′5″ (three-bay front) × 65′7½″ including rear additions, two-and-a-half stories on stone foundation, gable roof on main block, interior chimney on W., originally single room on each floor. Built c. 1832 by Samuel Fussell; extensive additions and interior alterations 20th C. 6 sheets (1975, including plans, elevations).

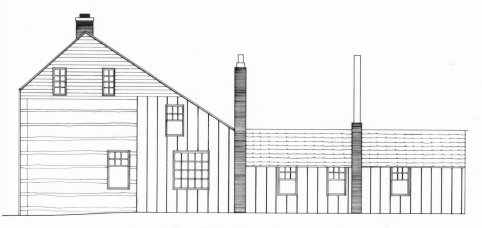

Samuel Fussell Log House, west elevation

Pennville   **Wayne County (89)**

Coffee Pot Restaurant (IN-120), N. side U.S. Rt. 40 (National Road), E. edge of Pennville. One-story commercial building with hipped roof, form-stone veneer, altered fenestration. Principally interesting for large coffee pot that rises from roof above central entrance. A good example of this genre of whimsical commercial architecture. 2 ext. photos (1975).

Ames-Paton House (IN-34), Waverly Rd. (County Rd. 150N), 2 mi. N.
of Pinola. Oak frame with clapboarding, 36′8″ (five-bay front) ×
26′6″ with a 36′ × 14′ one-story kitchen wing at W. side, one-and-a-
half stories, center door with transom, gable roof with later dormers
on N., central chimney plan. Built 1842 by Capt. Charles Ames of
Plymouth, Maine; reminiscent of austere 18th C. New England
farmhouses; 1838 wooden barn and 1856 residence of Ames' son
stand approx. 80 yds. from main house. 3 sheets (1955, including
site plan, plans, elevations, sections, details); 3 ext. photos (1956, including one of son's house), 5 int. photos (1956, including woodshed
and barn framing); 3 data pages (1957); HABSI form (1956).

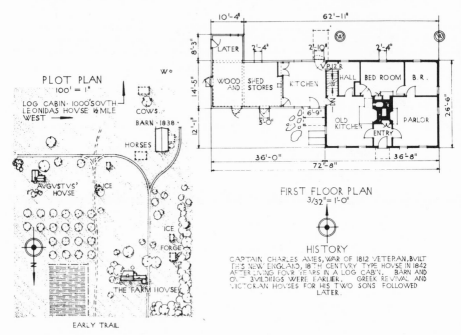

Ames-Paton House, portion of HABS sheet 1

Augsburg Swensk Skola (Burstrom Chapel) (IN-48), N. side Oak Hill
Rd., approx. 0.1 mi. E. of intersection U.S. Rt. 12. Frame with clap-

Augsburg Swensk Skola

boarding, 14'6" × 20'6", gable roof, one-room plan, battered bell tower (10'5" square at base) located off-center at rear. Built as a tool shed; given 1880 by Frederick Burstrom to Augsburg Congregation (Swedish Lutheran) for use as school; moved to Augsburg Cemetery and altered to accommodate school; operated until 1885; then used as Swedish-language summer school for several years; rededicated 1930 as Burstrom Chapel; still used by Augsburg Church; renovated 1970, adaptation of Scandinavian church architecture. 3 sheets (1964, including site plan, plan, elevations); 3 ext. photos (1963), 1 int. photo (1963); 3 data pages (1964).

Bailly, Joseph, Homestead (IN-42), N. side Howe Road, at Little Calumet River, now in Indiana Dunes National Lakeshore. This complex of buildings now maintained by the National Park Service was the trading post built 1822 by French trader Honoré Gratien Joseph Bailly de Messein at crossing of two Indian trails and a canoe route. Complex consists of two log structures built c. 1822 by Bailly; family house begun c. 1835 and continuously altered until 1917; brick structure c. 1880; two-story log servants' house c. 1900; restoration in progress. 3 data pages (1955); HABSI form (1957). NHL NR

Adams, Richard, House (IN-111), private road 0.6 mi. S. of U.S. Rt. 227. Brick, L-shaped, 44'4" (five-bay front) × 61', one-and-a-half stories, gable roofs with segmental dormers, shed-roof addition across rear, one-story extension on ell, porch along E. side ell; main entry has straight transom and sidelights with flanking pilasters; central hall plan; Greek Revival style; Ionic-order mantels and trim in front parlors; E. parlor has built-in sideboard; late Federal style trim in stairhall. Probably built between c. 1830 and 1843 as a dower house; restored 1975–76. 6 ext. photos (1975), 3 int. photos (1975); 4 data pages (1974).

Bethel A. M. E. Church

Bethel A. M. E. Church (IN-112), 200 S. 6th St., SW. corner S. 6th and B Sts. Brick with stone trim painted white, modified Greek cross plan, 55'6" (E. front) × 122'6", one story with basement, gable roofs, lower shed-roof additions in rear, square tower in NE. angle, triple stained-glass windows on N., S., and E. faces. Built 1857 by German Methodist congregation as simple rectangular building with Greek Revival details; purchased 1869 by Bethel A. M. E. Church; greatly altered and enlarged 1892 into present Romanesque Revival structure; further additions at rear to provide office space. Oldest black Methodist congregation in the state; founded 1836 by William Paul Quinn, early bishop of the A. M. E. church who organized over 50 churches in Midwest. A later pastor was James M. Townsend, who served as Recorder of Deeds in Washington, D.C., under President Benjamin Harrison and was the first black to serve in the Indiana legislature. 5 ext. photos (1975), 2 int. photos (1975); 11 data pages (1974). NR

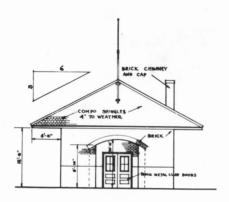

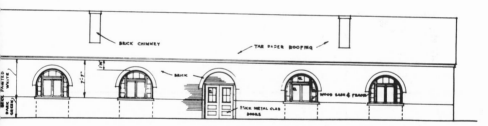

City Market (Richmond), east *(top)* and north elevations

City Market (IN-14), S. side Sixth St., at A St. Brick, 100'5" (five-bay front) × 24'2", one story (12' high), simple gable roof with 6' overhang on N. and S. sides, five arched doorways on long sides partially bricked in to form windows, interior one large undivided space. Built 1855; James M. Smith, architect; John A. McMinn, builder; demolished c. 1965. 3 sheets (1934, including plan, elevation, details); 2 ext. photos (1934); 2 data pages (1934).

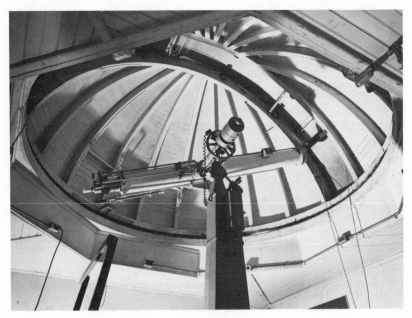

Earlham College Observatory

Earlham College Observatory (IN-113), Earlham College Campus, 65′ N. of Carpenter Hall (Administration Building). Simple brick building on limestone foundation, central square with slightly lower wings centered on E. and W. sides, 40′ × 17′, one story, low-hipped roofs, rotating observation dome over central block, covered opening for transit telescope in roof of W. wing. Interior comprises three interconnecting rooms; central room contained principal telescope; W. room originally housed transit telescope acquired 1861 from U.S. Coast Guard. Built 1860–61; probably first observatory at an Indiana college and one of earliest in the Midwest. 1 ext. photo (1975), 2 int. photos (1975); 5 data pages (1974).

Harrison, Thomas, House (IN-146), 514 W. Main St. Built 1885; attributed to Thomas Harrison, architect; demolished 1979. 7 sheets (1979, including site plan, plans, elevation, section, details); 7 ext. photos (1979), 13 int. photos (1979); 7 data pages (1979).

Hicksite Friends Meeting House (IN-119), 1150 North A St. Museum of Wayne County Historical Society. Brick, stone trim, five-bay front, one-and-a-half stories on raised basement, gable roof with cross gable above central entrance, paired windows articulated by recessed segmental wall arches, wooden porches, interior division for men and women now removed. Built 1865; interior altered for museum use. 1 ext. photo (1975). NR

Raukoph House (IN-118), 240 S. Third St. Brick, 26' (two-bay front) × 55'6" (including rear additions), one-and-a-half stories with one-story shed-roof rear additions, gable roof on main block with gable end to street, cornice returns, wooden side porch. Built sometime between 1851 and 1858; example of small but well-constructed cottages built by German immigrants to Richmond. See also records, including plans and elevations filed under Working-Class Houses (IN-116), Richmond. 2 ext. photos (1975), 2 int. photos (1975); 7 data pages (1974). NR (Old Richmond Historic District)

Scott, Andrew F., House (IN-145), 126 N. Tenth St. Owned by Wayne County Historical Society, under restoration as historic house museum. Brick, cubical with front-projecting pedimented pavilion and rear kitchen ell, three-bay front, two stories, hipped roof with elaborate cupola, recessed main entrance with engaged square piers, verandas flanking central pavilion, paired segmental arched windows above entry, deep cornice with decorative brackets; central hall plan with carved woodwork and marble fireplaces, original furniture; mid-19th C. Italianate details. Built 1858. 7 ext. photos (1975); 6 data pages (1974). NR

Starr Historic District Study (IN-114), bounded by North A, Tenth, North D, and Thirteenth Sts. Cohesive district of mid- and late 19th C. houses built on land owned by Charles Starr and subdivided by his heirs. Most houses brick, two stories, rectangular, with hipped roofs and Italianate trim consisting of decorative window hoods and bracketed cornices; some earlier houses show transitional Greek Revival details; general lack of elaborate ornamentation reflects influence of Quaker merchants and manufacturers who built most of houses; district contains a number of double houses and identical houses built side by side. Most construction took place between 1865 and 1870; some new construction and much remodeling—including addition of dark oak interior trim and exterior columnar porches—in late 19th and early 20th C.; remained fashionable residential neighborhood until early 20th C., when most houses were divided into apartments. Some important houses include the Scott House (IN-145), being restored by the Wayne County Historical Society, least altered of all houses in the district, simple Italianate trim with cupola, original furnishings; the Mendenhall-Reeves House (222 N.

Tenth St.), Italianate mansion with elaborate brackets and notable interior plasterwork; the Knights of Columbus Headquarters (204 N. Tenth St.), example of late 19th C. construction in the district. 35 ext. photos (1975, including 7 of 126 N. Tenth St., 6 of 204 N. Tenth St., and 6 of 222 N. Tenth St.), 5 int. photos (1975, including 2 of 204 N. Tenth, and 3 of 222 N. Tenth), 2 photocopies of map (1874); 22 data pages (1974). NR

Wayne County Courthouse (IN-115), occupies block bounded by Main and South A Sts., Third and Fourth Sts. Brick masonry with rock-faced Indiana limestone veneer, U-shaped with small court between legs of U, 214' (eleven-bay front) × 128', three-and-a-half stories on basement (exposed in rear), complex roof with cross gables intersecting hipped roofs, gabled wall dormers, octagonal tower on NE. corner, arcaded windows on second story, principal entry in projecting gabled pavilion on E., main stair with three-story open well, paneled courtrooms on third floor, marble wainscoting, oak trim, stained-glass transoms, Richardsonian Romanesque style. Built 1890–93; James McLaughlin, Cincinnati, architect; Aaron and Edwin Campfield, contractors; basically unaltered. Fifth courthouse to be erected in the county; good example of Indiana tradition of large, well-designed county courthouses; remodeled 1978. 17 ext. photos (1975), 11 int. photos (1975), photocopy of original rendering (c. 1890); 16 data pages (1974). NR

Working-Class Houses (IN-116), various locations Richmond, predominately on S. side of city in subdivisions adjacent to original plat. A comparative study of the small, gabled one-and-a-half-story cottages built in Richmond in mid-19th C., mostly by German immigrants. Though modest, most cottages were very well built, often by their occupants, many of whom were laborers and artisans. Houses are brick and frame and may be one-family or double houses. Small size requires compact and often ingenious plans, usually with side hall. Numerous examples, with a variety of exterior trim, exist in Richmond and surrounding towns. 2 sheets (1974, including site plan and elevations of four adjacent cottages at 230–240 S. Third St. and floor plans of the Raukoph House at 240 S. Third); 17 ext. photos (1975), 2 photocopies of maps (1854, 1874); 12 data pages (1974, general discussion of working-class cottages, including a chart locating and dating some of the most important examples). See also entry for Raukoph House (IN-118). NR (Old Richmond Historic District)

Starr Historic District Study

Wayne County Courthouse

Working-Class Houses (Richmond)

Ridgeville   **Randolph County (68)**

Ridgeville Switching Station (IN-158), East Rd., N. of State Rt. 28, N. side Pennsylvania R.R. (now Conrail) tracks opposite Ridgeville Station. Frame with clapboarding, 14′4″ × 37′5″, two stories, hipped roof. Built early 20th C.; demolished 1972. 6 sheets (n.d., including site plan, plan, elevations, details).

Rushville   **Rush County (70)**

Melodeon Hall (IN-97), 132–138 W. Second St., NE. corner W. Second and N. Morgan Sts. Brick, 82′ (twelve-bay front) × 72′ (four bays), two stories, sloping roof, designed to accommodate four stores (each three bays) on first floor and large hall on second floor, arcaded windows with keystones and impost blocks, modillion cornice, entrance to second-story hall on W. side, proscenium on curving E. wall (stage removed), commercial Italianate style. Built 1872; two shopfronts altered; small stage in hall added during World War II. A combination commercial building and hall similar to those built 19th

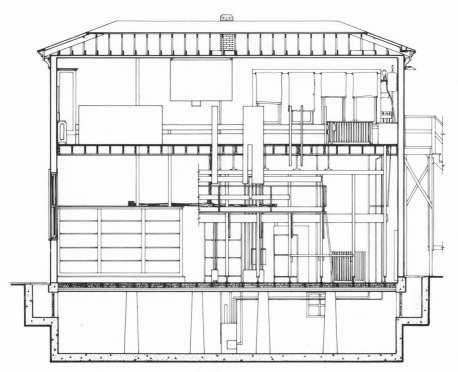

Ridgeville Switching Station, longitudinal section

Melodeon Hall, second-floor hall

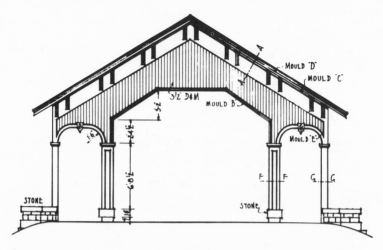

Kennedy Covered Bridge, west elevation

C. in many Indiana towns; used for cultural, social, and political affairs; served for a time as a nickelodeon. 3 ext. photos (1975), 2 int. photos (1975); 5 data pages (1974). NR

Rushville Vicinity   **Rush County (70)**

Kennedy Covered Bridge (IN-1), spanning Flat Rock River, State Rt. 44, 1 mi. E. of Rushville. Timber covered bridge, Burr truss construction, 166' span × 26' width, center roadway with pedestrian path on each side. Built 1880 by Everett L. Kennedy and C. F. Kennedy; destroyed 1960s. 7 sheets (1934, including plans, elevations, sections, details); 1 data page (1934).

Salem   **Washington County (88)**

Morrison, John I., House. See Old Salem School (IN-25), Salem.

Old Salem School (John Hay Birthplace) (IN-25), 106 S. College Ave. Historic house museum of Washington County Historical Society. Brick, 31' (three-bay front) × 60' with later addition, one story, gable roof, Federal style. Built 1824 as school; additions to rear 1843; restored 1971. Served as school of John Morrison, pioneer Indiana educator. Birthplace of John Milton Hay (1838–1905), Civil

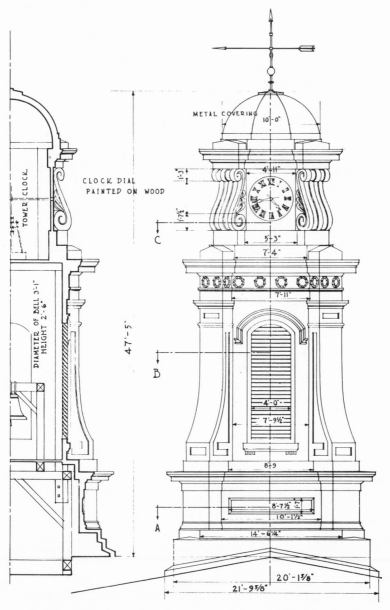

METAL COVERING 10'-0"

CLOCK DIAL
PAINTED ON WOOD

TOWER CLOCK

DIAMETER OF BELL 3'-1"
HEIGHT 2'-6"

47'-5"

C

B

A

1'-3"

1'-7½"

4'-11"

5'-3"

7'-4"

7'-11"

4'-0"

7'-9½"

8'-9

8'-7½"

10'-1½"

14'-6¼"

20'-1⅝"

21'-9⅝"

Second St. Joseph County Courthouse, tower details

War secretary to President Abraham Lincoln and U.S. Secretary of State under Presidents William McKinley and Theodore Roosevelt. 4 sheets (1936, including plan, elevations, details). NR

South Bend   **St. Joseph County (71)**

Second St. Joseph County Courthouse (IN-12), originally at SW. corner Main St. and Washington Ave., now at 112 S. Lafayette Blvd. Museum of Northern Indiana Historical Society. Brick faced with limestone, 61'2" (three-bay front) × 89' (five bays), two stories on raised basement, two-story portico at W., low gable roof with elaborate wooden clock tower, six portico columns plastered brick with pseudo-Corinthian caps, Greek Revival style, central hall plan, office on main floor. Courtroom remodeled 1873; building moved 1895–96 to present location; first floor altered 1907 for museum use. 12 sheets (1934, including plans, elevations, section, details); 3 ext. photos (1934), 2 data pages (1934); HABSI form (1970). NR

Turkey Run State Park   **Parke County (61)**

Narrows Covered Bridge (IN-159), spanning Sugar Creek, at E. edge of park. Frame with vertical siding, 145'7½" × 19'6", single span, limestone abutments, Burr arch trusses. Built 1882 by Joseph A. Britton, a Parke County native. First of at least 23 bridges, possibly as many as 40, that Britton and his sons built in Parke and surrounding counties. 5 sheets (n.d., including plans, elevations, sections). NR (Parke County Covered Bridges Multiple Resource Area)

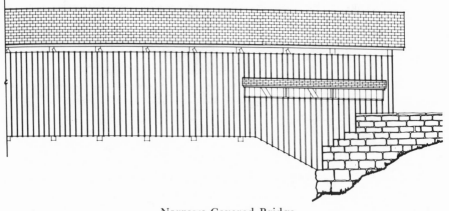

Narrows Covered Bridge

John Francis Dufour House, riverfront elevation

Vevay **Switzerland County (78)**

Dufour, John Francis, House (Ferry House) (IN-16), between Walnut and Ferry Sts., on Ohio River. Fieldstone, 72′3″ × 20′6″, two-and-a-half-story main block and one-story kitchen joined by two-story frame addition, gable roofs, two-story porch at S. (river) front with wooden columns and straight-run exterior stair. Built 1811 by John Francis Dufour, one of Swiss settlers who founded Vevay; demolished 1962. Called Ferry House because of service as inn for river travelers. 3 sheets (1934, including plans, elevations); 3 ext. photos (1934, n.d.); 2 data pages (1934); HABSI form (1962).

Ruter Chapel (Methodist) (IN-27), 309 W. Main St., at Union St. Brick, 45′ (three-bay front) × 70′ (five bays), two stories with auditorium above church schoolrooms, gable roof with octagonal wooden bell tower, simple facade pedimented with four Doric pilasters over an exposed basement containing central double-door entry, Greek Revival style, chancel and organ panel with carved wooden trim of Classical design. Built 1859. 6 sheets (1936, including plans, elevations, section, details).

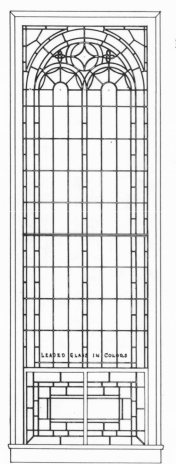

Ruter Chapel, second-floor
window

LEADED GLASS IN COLORS

Ruter Chapel, organ panel trim

Ulysses P. Schenck House, north porch details

Schenck, Ulysses P., House (IN-28), 630 W. Market St., on Ohio River. Brick, 46' (three-bay front) × 49'4", two-and-a-half stories, basement exposed on S., hipped roof with cupola, two-story Ionic portico on S. (river) side, one-story Ionic porch on N. facade, cast-iron railings; main entrance has later beveled glass in door, lights, and transom; door to balcony above has early tracery in transom and side lights; central hall plan; freestanding spiral stair from first floor to cupola; Greek Revival style. Built 1840–45 for Ulysses P. Schenck, flatboat magnate; George H. Kyle, architect; stair by Francis Costigan. 10 sheets (1936, including plans, elevations, details); HABSI form (1957).

Switzerland County Courthouse Privy (IN-80), near SE. corner intersection Pike and Main Cross Sts., NW. of courthouse. Brick, one-story, hexagonal, standing seam metal roof with small louvered cupola in center. Probably built c. 1864. 2 ext. photos (1971).

Switzerland County Courthouse Privy

Michael Brouillet House

Basilica of Saint Francis Xavier. See Saint Francis Xavier Cathedral (IN-7), Vincennes.

Brouillet, Michael, House (Old French House) (IN-160), 509 N. First St. Frame with clapboarding, 39'3" (three-bay front) × 29'3", one-and-a-half stories, low-pitched gable roof forms broad apron porches on E. and W., E. and W. walls stuccoed, large stone fireplace on N, wall with interior and exterior hearth. Built c. 1806 by French fur trader Michael Brouillet; of French Colonial style more common in the southern U.S.; sole surviving known example in Indiana of 18th C. French *poteaux-sur-sole* (post-on-foundation) construction; restored 1979–80. 4 data pages (1975). NR (Vincennes Historic District)

College of Vincennes, Saint Rose Chapel (now Saint Francis Xavier, Saint Rose Chapel) (IN-74), S. side Second St., between Church and Barnett Sts. Brick, one story, gable roof over main portion, shed-roof addition at N., rudimentary temple front with center door and four engaged Doric pilasters in brick on S. elevation, oculus window in gable. Originally part of the seminary of College of Vincennes. 1 ext. photo (1934); HABSI form (1970). NR (Old Cathedral Complex)

"Grouseland" (William Henry Harrison House) (IN-17), NW. corner Park and Scott Sts. Historic house museum of Daughters of the American Revolution. Brick, 55' (five-bay front) × 72', two-and-a-half-story main block with one-and-a-half-story kitchen to N. linked by one-story addition, hipped roof on main block, W. wall of main block forming large curved bay, central hall plan, curving wooden staircase. Built 1803–04 for William Henry Harrison, governor of the Northwest Territory; William Lindsey, builder. Served dual role as territorial governor's mansion and military headquarters; room to W. of hall was council chamber. 9 sheets (1934, including plans, elevations, details); 2 ext. photos (1934), 4 int. photos (1934); 24 data pages (1930, 1934); HABSI form (1953). NHL NR

Harrison, William Henry, House. See "Grouseland" (IN-17), Vincennes.

Old French House. See Brouillet, Michael, House (IN-160), Vincennes.

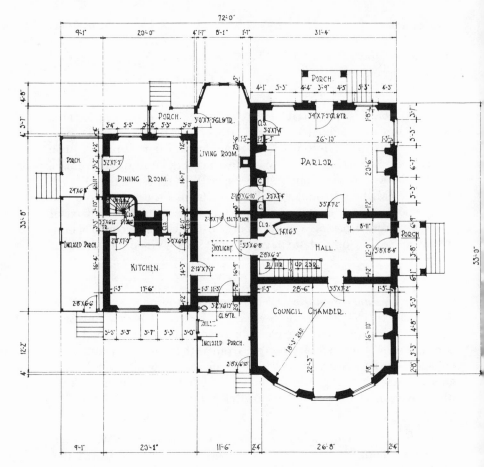

"Grouseland," first-floor plan

Saint Francis Xavier Cathedral (now Basilica of Saint Francis Xavier) (IN-7), W. side Church St., between Second St. and Memorial Dr. Brick, Flemish bond, 60′6″ (three-bay front) × 125′5″ (five bays plus apse), 102′-high wood-framed tower with galvanized iron trim; tower straddles ridge at E. end of gable roof; pedimented facade has three semicircular arched doorways with corresponding arched sculptural niches above; brick buttresses separate bays on side elevations; large wooden Doric columns divide nave from aisles; semicircular chancel at W.; wooden balcony at E. end of nave; painted canvas ceiling; crypt below apse. Built 1826–36 under Bishop Simon Brute. First cathedral church in Indiana; elevated to minor basilica

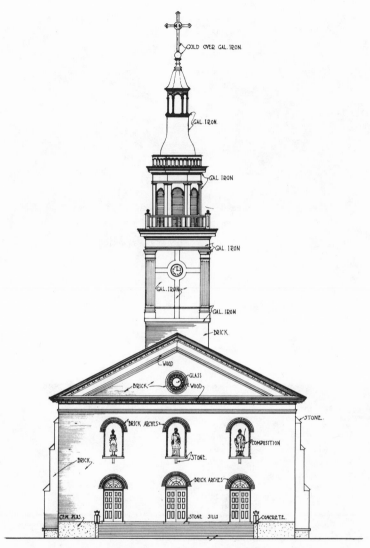

Saint Francis Xavier Cathedral, north elevation

1970. 22 sheets (1934, including plans, elevations, sections, details); 2 ext. photos (1934), 1 int. photo (1934); 2 data pages (1934). NR (Old Cathedral Complex)

Saint Francis Xavier, Library (IN-75), W. side Church St., S. of Saint Francis Xavier Cathedral. Brick, 36′ (three-bay front) × 14′, one

Ranck Round Barn

Ranck Round Barn, interior roof structure

story on high basement, hipped roof, round-arch openings, center doors E. and W. with semicircular fanlights, Classical Revival design. Built 1840 for Bishop de la Hailandiere; books moved to new library across courtyard to W. and building renovated as museum shop 1968. Earliest library building in the state. 1 ext. photo (1934); HABSI form (1970). NR (Old Cathedral Complex)

Saint Francis Xavier, Priests' House (IN-76), NW. corner Second and Church Sts. Brick, three-bay front, two-and-a-half stories on raised basement, hipped roof, brick cornice; main door has straight transom and sidelights. Built c. 1840; two-story kitchen addition to W. in 20th C. Serves as residence and refectory. 1 ext. photo (1934). NR (Old Cathedral Complex)

Saint Francis Xavier, Saint Rose Chapel. See College of Vincennes, St. Rose Chapel (IN-74), Vincennes.

Waterloo Vicinity   Fayette County (21)

Ranck Round Barn (McDivitt Round Barn) (IN-106), Fayette-Wayne County Line Rd. (500N), 0.5 mi. W. of intersection Willow Grove Rd. (County Rd. 350W), 3.5 mi. NE. of Waterloo. Frame with vertical siding, round , 70' in diameter at base, 70' high, two stories with clerestory and round lantern, conical roofs of decreasing size; main entrance to second-floor storage area has shallow projecting gable and is approached by earthen ramp; first-floor entrance for livestock; intricate framing of many small timber members with no central support. Built sometime between 1885 and 1910, perhaps by Isaac McNammee of Knightstown, Indiana, who took out a patent on a "self-supporting conical roof" in 1905. One of the most elaborate of a number of round barns built in eastern Indiana approx. same time. 6 ext. photos (1975), 2 int. photos (1975); 7 data pages (1974).

Westfield   Hamilton County (29)

Doan House. See Conner Prairie Pioneer Settlement, Doan House (IN-96), Noblesville.

Appendix A: Historic American Buildings Survey Inventory (HABSI) in Indiana

Aurora   **Dearborn County (15)**

"Hillforest" (Thomas Gaff House), 213 Fifth St. Historic house museum of Hillforest Historical Foundation, Inc. Frame, stuccoed and scored to resemble stone, 79' (five-bay front) × 63', two stories with basement and three-story service ell, semicircular portico topped by circular belvedere, central hall plan, wide dog-leg stair, parquet floors, ornamental iron fireplaces, painted plasterwork. Built 1852–56 for Thomas Gaff, pioneer Indiana and Ohio industrialist; 1870 Eastlake room added above service wing; restored 1969. HABSI forms (1956, 1970). NR

Bloomington   **Monroe County (53)**

Woodburn-Wells House, 519 N. College Ave. Brick, three-bay facade, two stories with two-story side gallery (enclosed) on rear ell, gable roofs, side hall plan. Built 1829–31 by Charles Woodburn; occupied 1932–57 by Herman B Wells, president of Indiana University 1937–62. HABSI form (1958).

Bloomington Vicinity   **Monroe County (53)**

Stout, Daniel, House ("Old Stone House on the Hill"), U.S. Rt. 46, 3 mi. N. of Bloomington, on W. side of Maple Grove Rd. Limestone walls 22" thick, three-bay symmetrical facade, two stories, gable roof, stone gable-end chimneys. Built 1828 by Daniel Stout. Oldest house still standing in Monroe County. HABSI form (1958). NR

Bluffton   **Wells County (90)**

Wells County Courthouse, SW. corner Main and Market Sts. Tan sandstone, two-and-a-half stories on a raised basement, asymmetrical composition with five-story clock tower at NE. corner, Richardsonian Romanesque style. Built 1888–91; George W. Bunting and Son, architects. HABSI form (1970). NR

Brookville Vicinity   **Franklin County (24)**

Little Cedar Grove Baptist Church, E. side U.S. Rt. 52, 3 mi. S. of Brookville.
Museum. Brick, rectangular, approx. 35' (three-bay front) × approx. 22',
one-and-a-half stories, gable roof, balcony, charcoal burning pit with no
chimney. Built 1812; restored 1915, 1946, 1955. Oldest church in the state
still in original location. HABSI form (1962).

Chesterton Vicinity   **Porter County (64)**

Baileytown School, District No. 5, Old Baileytown Rd., at SW. corner section 28.
Brick with limestone keystone and sills, 50' (three-bay front) × 28', one
story, gable roof with bracketed front gable, one room plan. Built 1885;
Nathan Demass, builder. Demolished c. 1965. Typical one-room
schoolhouse. HABSI form (1964).

Connersville   **Fayette County (21)**

Smith, Oliver H., House ("Elmhurst," now Warren Lodge No. 15), W. side S.
Central Ave., S. of Third St. Brick, five-bay main block with three-bay wings
at N. and S., two stories, two-story hexastyle portico on E., gable roof, Greek
Revival style, interior cherry and oak paneling added c. 1850. Built 1831 for
Oliver H. Smith; remodeled c. 1850, 1881, c. 1910, after 1940. HABSI form
(1958). NR

Connersville Vicinity   **Fayette County (21)**

Gray House (IN-108). See full HABS entry.

Crawfordsville   **Montgomery County (54)**

Lane, Henry S., House ("Lane Place"), E. side Water St., between Pike and
Wabash Sts. Historic house museum of Montgomery County Historical Society. Brick, five-bay facade, two stories with two-story Doric portico, low-
pitched hipped roof, central hall plan. Built c. 1835 as two-room, one-story
house of W. P. Hawkins; enlarged 1845 by Henry S. Lane, a founder of the
Republican Party, U.S. Senator, and confidant of Abraham Lincoln; remodeled and additions to E. and N. 1935. HABSI form (1957).

Crown Point   **Lake County (45)**

Lake County Courthouse, Courthouse Square, W. side Main St., between Clark
and E. Joliet Sts. Brick, two stories on raised basement, three Greek cross-
shaped units, central unit crowned with clock tower, side units (N. and S.)

with smaller cupolas, arms of cross organized as pedimented facades with corner pilasters. Central portion built 1878–79; John C. Cochrane, architect; N. and S. wings added 1907 by Beers and Beers, architects; one-story extensions added 1928 by Beers and Beers. Adapted for commercial use. HABSI form (1970). NR

Dexter Vicinity   Perry County (62)

Springer, Joseph, House, E. side State Rt. 66, 4 mi. N. of Dexter. Log covered with weatherboard and board and batten, two stories, two gable-roofed blocks end to end, two stone chimneys, simple spiral staircase, large fireplaces, handcarved mantels. Built 1831 by the Reverend Joseph Springer, Methodist circuit minister. Served as residence, church, and general store. Now ruins. HABSI form (1962).

Evansville   Vanderburgh County (82)

Heilman, William, House (now St. Vincent's Day Nursery), 611 First Ave. Brick, three-bay main facade faced with stone, two stories, flat roof, Renaissance Revival style. Built 1869 for William Heilman; Henry Mursinna, architect. HABSI form (1970).

Viele, Charles, House, 404 SE. Riverside Dr. (originally 906 Water St.). Brick with metal cornice and window frames, five-bay front, two-and-a-half stories with mansard roof, two-story cast-iron entrance porch. Built 1855 for Charles Viele; remodeled by Viele 1872; restored 1960s by Lewis J. Kock, Jr. Originally two-story, four-gable house of Italianate design; remodeled in Second Empire style. HABSI form (1970).

Willard Library, 21 First Ave. Brick with wooden framing, limestone trim, two stories with raised stone basement, entrance tower on SW. corner, hipped roof, carved Ruskinian Gothic details. Begun 1877; Boyd and Brickley, architects. Redesigned and completed 1882–84; Reid Brothers, architects. Few alterations to original fabric. Land and money provided by prominent business leader and philanthropist Willard Carpenter. HABSI form (1970). NR

Finley Vicinity   Shelby County (73)

Copple, Daniel, House ("Rosewell"), SE. corner County Rds. 900N and 200W, off U.S. 52, 4 mi. S. of center of Finley. Frame, 32' (six-bay facade), one-and-a-half stories, gable roof with one-story Doric distyle porch, Greek Revival style. Built c. 1835 by Daniel Copple; restored and rooms added to E. c. 1955; restored 1974 after storm damage. HABSI form (1959).

Fountain City   Wayne County (89)

Coffin, Levi, House (IN-79). See full HABS entry.

Greensburg   Decatur County (16)

Decatur County Courthouse, N. side W. Main St., at Broadway. Brick with stone trim, stuccoed since 1903, thirteen bays × three bays, two stories with four- and five-story towers, gable roofs, elaborate skyline, arcuated fenestration, crenelated tower, Romanesque Revival style. Built 1854–60; Edwin May, architect; interior remodeled 1890. Admired by William Jennings Bryan and made famous as "tree in the tower" courthouse by William Allen White. HABSI form (1970). NR

Hanover   Jefferson County (39)

Crowe, John Finley, House, NW. corner Crowe St. and Presbyterian Ave., N. of Hanover Presbyterian Church. Wooden frame, seven-bay front, including wings, two-story main block with one-story wings, gable roof, two-story gallery across main block. Built 1829. On the site of original building of Hanover Academy, later Hanover College. HABSI form (1962).

Hanover College YMCA Building, Hanover College Campus, originally on mall at S. end Lucina Ball Dr., now on W. side Lucina Ball Dr., 2 blocks N. of Prospect St. Wooden frame, 24′4″ (one-bay front) × 42′5″ (four bays), gable roof. Built 1883. First campus YMCA in U.S. HABSI form (1962).

Hobart Vicinity   Lake County (45)

Wolf, Josephus, House, Cleveland St., 4.5 mi. E. of Hobart. Brick farmhouse, two stories with cupola; main block contained family rooms and farm office, rear ell contained family and workmen's dining rooms, workmen's bedrooms, and carriage house; Italianate style. Built 1875; restored c. 1970 for commercial use. HABSI form (1970).

Indianapolis   Marion County (49)

Allison, James A., House ("Riverdale," now on Marian College Campus) (IN-68). See full HABS entry.

Bals-Wocher House (Record Data, Inc.), 951 N. Delaware St. Brick, four bays × four bays, two-and-a-half stories with basement, hipped roof, stone trim, quoining, arcuated porch, Italianate style, fine mantels and woodwork. Built 1869 for H. G. Bals; additions W. and N. after 1920; restored c. 1975; adapted for commercial use. HABSI form (1970). NR

Bates-Hendricks House (IN-64). See full HABS entry.

Benton House. See Ohmer-Benton House, Indianapolis.

Butler, David, House, 1306 N. Park Ave. Brick, three-bay facade, two-and-a-half stories, hipped and gable roofs, 25 rooms, 12 fireplaces with trim of wood, marble slate, and tile. Built 1848 for David Butler, president of Northwestern Christian University; extensive alterations and additions c. 1890; restored 1978–79 as apartments. HABSI form (1957).

Christ (Episcopal) Church (IN-103). See full HABS entry.

Fletcher, Albert E., Mansion, 1121 N. Pennsylvania St. Brick, five-bay front, two-and-a-half stories, low-hipped roof, heavy bracketed cornice with attic windows in frieze, corner quoins, projecting entrance pavilion, balcony over main entry, Italianate style, elaborately carved fireplaces. Built 1873–76; Joseph Curzon, architect. Demolished 1960s. HABSI form (1957).

Harrison, Benjamin, House (IN-53). See full HABS entry.

Indiana Central State Hospital, Pathological Department Building (IN-69). See full HABS entry.

Julian, George W., House, 115 S. Audubon Rd. Brick, two stories, low-pitched hipped roof, bracketed cornice, frame porch, ornamental arched window lintels, Italianate style. Built 1873–76 for George W. Julian, U.S. Congressman and humanitarian; remodeled before 1960 as a sanitarium. HABSI form (1960).

Morris-Butler House (IN-52). See full HABS entry.

Nickum, John R., House (James Whitcomb Riley House) (IN-51). See full HABS entry.

Ohmer-Benton House, 312 S. Downey Ave. Museum of Irvington Historic Landmarks Foundation; clubhouse for Irvington-area organizations. Brick, 34' × 52', one story with mansard, asymmetrical plan with tower entry and projecting polygonal bays at N. and S., fine woodwork and oak flooring. Built 1873 by Nickolas Ohmer; restored 1966–67. Occupied 1890–1907 by Allen R. Benton, president of Butler University. HABSI forms (1967, 1970). NR

Old Federal Building, 45 N. Pennsylvania St. Brick and limestone, 70' (five-bay front) × 90', three stories with one-story portico on Pennsylvania St., low-pitched hipped roof screened by stone balustrade, rusticated ground floor, Neoclassical details. Built 1856–61; A. B. Young, architect. Enlarged 1873–74; A. B. Mullett, architect. Demolished 1963. HABSI form (1963).

Second Presbyterian Church, NW. corner Vermont and Pennsylvania Sts. Limestone, one story with basement and balcony, gable roof, main tower at SE. 161' high, chapel tower 96' high, Gothic Revival style, auditorium and chapel major spaces, interior woodwork black walnut. Built 1866–70; Joseph Curzon, architect. Demolished 1960. HABSI form (1962).

Ball, James, Homestead, 1202 Columbia St. Brick with limestone trim on a raised basement exposed in rear, three-bay facade, two stories, gable roof, gable end to street, carved wooden brackets, side hall plan, cherry staircase and carved mantels. Built 1862 by James Ball. Restored 1969; H. Roll McLaughlin, architect. HABSI form (1970).

Fowler, Moses, House, 909 South St. Historic house museum of Tippecanoe County Historical Association. Stuccoed brick, asymmetrical L-shaped plan, two-and-a-half stories, gable roof with cross gables and wall dormers, Gothic Revival style, fine carved woodwork and plaster ceilings. Built 1850–52 by Moses Fowler, wealthy canal merchant, from designs in A. J. Downing publication; remodeled and addition made to SE. 1916. HABSI form (1970). NR

Tippecanoe County Courthouse, Public Square, Fourth St., between Main and Columbia Sts. Limestone, two-and-a-half stories on raised basement, tall central metal dome, cross plan, eight pavilion blocks (two bracketing temple fronts on each of four faces), Second Empire style. Built 1881–85; traditionally attributed to Elias Max, but may have been adaptation of designs submitted by James F. Alexander, superintendent of construction; courtrooms altered 1969. HABSI form (1970). NR

LaGrange   **LaGrange County (44)**

LaGrange County Courthouse, W. side Detroit St., between Michigan and Spring Sts. Brick with sandstone trim and metal cornices, five-bay front, two stories on raised basement, cross-gable roof with slate roofing, central clock tower and four corner tower-like pavilions, central hall plan, Renaissance Revival style. Built 1878; T. J. Tolan and Son, architects. HABSI form (1970).

La Porte   **La Porte County (46)**

La Porte County Courthouse, W. side Michigan St., between State St. and Lincolnway. Wisconsin sandstone, cross plan, three-and-a-half stories, gable roof with slate roofing, central clock tower, Richardsonian Romanesque style. Built 1892; Brentwood S. Tolan, architect. HABSI form (1970).

Lawrenceburg   **Dearborn County (15)**

Dearborn County Courthouse, N. side High St., between Charlotte and Mary Sts. Limestone ashlar, five-bay front × eight bays, three stories with first floor treated as heavy basement, Corinthian tetrastyle portico at S., Neoclassical style. Built 1870–71; George Kyle, architect. HABSI form (1970).

Vance-Tousey House (now Lotus Warehouse), 508 W. High St. Brick, five bays, two-story main block with one-and-a-half-story wings forming open-end court on N., pediment with fanlight, arched doorway with Palladian window above on S., Federal style, spiral staircase. Built 1816 for Samuel C. Vance, founder of Lawrenceburg; stairway attributed to Francis Costigan; interior extensively remodeled for offices. HABSI form (1958).

Liberty   Union County (81)

Nixson, John S., House, 313 E. Union St. Wooden frame, two-and-a-half stories, gable roof, four-story tower containing main door and two-story stair hall, round-headed windows, bracketed eaves, tower flanked by one-story porches. Neo-Jacobean and Italianate details. Built 1879; remodeled and addition to N. 1950s; remodeled c. 1975 for use as medical facility. HABSI form (1963).

Madison   Jefferson County (39)

Lanier, James F. D., House (IN-23). See full HABS entry.

Shrewsbury, Charles L., House (IN-8). See full HABS entry.

Mays Vicinity   Rush County (70)

Hall, William, House, N. side Raleigh Rd., 2 mi. E. of Mays. Wooden frame, octagonal plan, two stories; one face is a two-story recessed porch with octagonal columns; low-pitched roof. Built 1855 by William Hall. Said to be first home in state built with precut members. Frank T. Hall, born here, became lieutenant governor of Indiana. HABSI form (1958).

Mount Auburn   Wayne County (89)

Huddleston House (IN-110). See full HABS entry.

Newburgh   Warrick County (87)

Bethell, Thomas F., House (Frank J. Folz, Jr., House), 6 Sycamore St. Brick with stone trim, five bays × two bays, two stories, one-story Doric distyle porch with entablature and balustrade, low-pitched cross-gable roof with paired decorative brackets, central hall plan, Classically detailed interior woodwork; vestibule doors have ovoid colored-glass lights. Built 1858–59 for Thomas Bethell; Noyes White, architect; Mr. Mackay, builder. HABSI form (1958).

Roberts, Gaines Hardy, House ("Old Stone House") (IN-13). See full HABS entry.

New Castle   **Henry County (33)**

Henry County Courthouse, W. side Main St., between Race and Broad Sts. Brick, limestone trim and quoining, two stories, clock tower at center of E. elevation, Italianate with Georgian details. Built 1866; Isaac Hodgson, architect. Size of building doubled by addition to W. in 1902. HABSI form (1970).

New Harmony   **Posey County (65)**

Log House (Macluria Double Log House), behind 324 North St. Museum. Hewn log construction, two one-story rooms with dogtrot between. Built early 19th C. on banks of nearby Wabash River; moved c. 1965 to S. Main St.; moved c. 1975 to present location; restored by Historic New Harmony, Inc. HABSI form (1970). NHL

Macluria Double Log House. See Log House, New Harmony.

Rappite House (David Lenz House), originally N. side Church St., between Main and Brewery Sts., now at 324 North St. Historic house museum. Frame, two stories, simple gable roof, rear shed addition. Built c. 1815; moved to present site 1961. Restored by National Society of Colonial Dames as typical example of Rappite frame construction. HABSI form (1970). NHL NR (New Harmony Historic District)

Noblesville   **Hamilton County (29)**

Stone, Judge Earl S., House, 107 S. Eighth St. Brick, five-bay front, two stories, gable roof; doorway has straight transom with sidelights; Greek Revival details. Built 1849. HABSI form (1972). NR

Noblesville Vicinity   **Hamilton County (29)**

Conner Prairie Pioneer Settlement, William Conner House (IN-46). See full HABS entry.

Paoli   **Orange County (59)**

Orange County Courthouse (IN-29). See full HABS entry.

Pinola Vicinity   **La Porte County (46)**

Ames-Paton House (IN-34). See full HABS entry.

Plymouth   **Marshall County (50)**

Marshall County Courthouse, Walnut St., between W. Madison and W. Jefferson Sts. Brick with stone trim and quoining, two stories, projecting Corinthian porticoes with entablatures at center of E. and W. facades, center of building marked by drum and dome with inset clock, Georgian Revival design. Built 1870; G. P. Randall, architect. Interior remodeled c. 1920. HABSI form (1970).

Porter Vicinity   **Porter County (64)**

Bailly, Joseph, Homestead (IN-42). See full HABS entry.

Rochester   **Fulton County (25)**

Fulton County Courthouse, E. side Main St., between 8th and 9th Sts. Quarry-faced stone, cross plan, two-and-a-half stories, hipped roof with gables and central clock tower, ten stone lions around building, Richardsonian Romanesque style. Built 1895; A. W. Rush and Son, architects. HABSI form (1970).

South Bend   **St. Joseph County (71)**

Second St. Joseph County Courthouse (IN-12). See full HABS entry.

Terre Haute   **Vigo County (84)**

Condit House. See Houriet, Lucien, House, Indiana State University, Terre Haute.

Dewees, Maj. George W., House (Nathaniel Preston House), 1339 Poplar St. Frame, one story with high basement typical of French Colonial architecture of southern U.S., wooden galleries on N. and S. supported by brick piers with stone caps, broad low-pitched gable roof covering rooms and galleries, central hall plan, fine interior woodwork and mantels. Possibly built before 1823 by Maj. George W. Dewees; purchased 1843 by Nathaniel Preston; damaged by fire 1980; to be restored. HABSI form (1958).

Houriet, Lucien, House (Condit House), facing main quadrangle on campus of Indiana State University. Brick, two stories, hipped roof, projecting entrance pavilion, bracketed cornice, Italianate style, Italian frescoed ceiling decoration added c. 1875. Built 1860 for Lucien Houriet, a jeweler; Jabez Hedden, builder; owned by Condit family 1863–1962. Restored and enlarged 1967–68 as home of university president; Roll McLaughlin, architect. HABSI form (1958). NR

Nathaniel Preston House. See Dewees, Maj. George W., House, Terre Haute.

Vernon   **Jennings County (40)**

Jennings County Courthouse, E. side Pike St., between Jackson (State Rt. 7) and Brown Sts. Brick, originally two stories, vermiculated limestone trim, tower at W. side, Italianate style. Built 1859; Isaac Hodgson, architect. Interior renovated mid-1950s when second story subdivided to make a third-story addition to N. HABSI form (1970). NR (Vernon Historic District)

Vevay   **Switzerland County (78)**

Dufour, John Francis, House (Ferry House) (IN-16). See full HABS entry.

Schenck, Ulysses P., House (IN-28). See full HABS entry.

Switzerland County Courthouse, N. side Main St., between Liberty and Main Cross Sts. Brick with stone trim, two stories with full exposed basement, gable roof with dome-and-drum clock tower at center, central N.-S. corridor, two-story courtroom at S. half of second floor, Greek Revival style. Hexagonal brick privy building (IN-80) to NW. Built 1864. HABSI form (1970).

Vevay Vicinity   **Switzerland County (78)**

Dufour, John David, House, N. side State Rt. 56, 1.5 mi. E. of Vevay. Wooden frame, 80′ (five-bay front with low symmetrical side wings) × 18′, 10′ × 10′ ell at NE., one-and-a-half stories, gable roofs, wooden porches at S. front and N. side of main block, four rooms in a row with central hall. Built 1813–26 by John David Dufour, one of the founders of Vevay; burned 1974. HABSI form (1963).

Wright, John W., House, N. side State Rt. 256, 3 mi. W. of Vevay. Wooden frame and brick, one-and-a-half stories, low-pitched gable roof, three-column porch at S. with roof balcony reached by Palladian doorway; unusual four-compartment plan suggests ship design; spiral staircase with flaring treads, interior woodwork has nautical details. Built 1836 for John W. Wright; C. B. Freeman and Son, architect-builders, were formerly shipwrights. HABSI form (1957).

126

College of Vincennes, Saint Rose Chapel (now Saint Francis Xavier, Saint Rose Chapel) (IN-75). See full HABS entry.

Ellis, Judge Abner T., Mansion (now Harmony Club), 111 N. Second St. Brick, two stories, three-bay sandstone facade with sandstone tetrastyle Tuscan portico, Greek Revival style. Built c. 1838 for Abner T. Ellis; John Moore, architect. Original one-story wing at rear now destroyed. First-floor interior extensively remodeled from 1938 on. HABSI from (1970). NR (Vincennes Historic District)

"Grouseland" (William Henry Harrison House) (IN-17). See full HABS entry.

Knox County Courthouse, SE. corner Seventh and Busseron Sts. Limestone, five-bay facade, three-and-a-half stories, dormered hipped roof, simple cross-axis plan with towers at four corners, Lombard Romanesque Revival style. Built 1873–74; Edwin May, architect; F. L. Farman, builder; renovated 1928. Built as a courthouse and a memorial to county soldiers and pioneers. HABSI form (1970). NR (Vincennes Historic District)

Saint Francis Xavier, Library (IN-76). See full HABS entry.

State Bank of Indiana (now Northwest Territory Art Guild), 112 N. Second St. Brick with stone trim, two stories, gable roof, limestone Doric tetrastyle portico; main banking space has bell dome of brick supported by six fluted Doric columns; Classical Revival style. Built 1838. Extensively restored 1964–66; H. Roll McLaughlin, architect. Highly successful bank associated with the expansion of the state 1834–58. HABSI form (1970). NR

Territory Hall, near intersection Park and Harrison Sts. Museum of the State of Indiana. Wooden frame, 26'2" × 19'7", two stories with one-story porch to E., gable roof, exterior stairway. Built c. 1800; restored 1933; moved 1949 to present site. (its fourth) Originally located on Main St. Served as first capitol of Northwest Territory. HABSI form (1970). NR

Warsaw   **Kosciusko County (43)**

Kosciusko County Courthouse, N. side Center St., between Buffalo and Lake Sts. Limestone, two stories with mansard on a raised basement, central clock tower, cross plan with corner pavilions, Second Empire style. Built 1882; T. J. Tolan and Son, architects. One of most elaborately ornamental and best-preserved courthouses in the state. HABSI form (1970).

West Baden Springs   **Orange County (59)**

West Baden Springs Hotel (now Northwood Institute), W. side State Rt. 56. Steel frame and concrete, six stories, 700 rooms; large glass-domed interior atrium, 195' in internal diameter, 150' high (six stories); dome supported by twenty-four steel-trussed radiating members and covered with glass skylight. Built 1901–02 for Col. Lee W. Sinclair; Harrison Albright, architect; Oliver H. Westcott, engineer, designed the dome. Renovated 1917 after fire and most of present interior decoration added, including mosaic tile floor. Altered 1930s; exterior ornament removed when used as a Jesuit monastery. Built in area famous for mineral springs; attracted a colorful clientele. HABSI form (1962). HAER NR

Appendix B: Historic American Engineering Record (HAER) in Indiana

Alamo Vicinity (Deer Mill)   **Montgomery County (54)**

Deer Mill Covered Bridge (HAER IN-28), spanning Sugar Creek, 500' W. of State Rt. 234, 2.5 mi. S. of Alamo. Frame with vertical siding, stone abutments, two spans, Burr arch trusses. Built 1878; Joseph J. Daniels, builder. 5 sheets (1974, site, plan, sections, elevations).

Alton Vicinity   **Crawford County (13)**

Mill Creek Bridge (HAER IN-23), spanning Mill Creek, 0.5 mi. N. of Alton. Iron, single span, Pratt through-truss. Built 1885; Indianapolis Bridge Co., builder. 7 ext. photos (1974).

Anderson   **Madison County (48)**

Anderson Carriage Manufacturing Company (HAER IN-37), NW. corner 25th and Walton Sts. Built c. 1900; partially destroyed c. 1935 by fire. Produced carriages and buggies; later manufactured Anderson automobile 1908–10. 1 sheet (1972, plans, elevations); 1 photocopy of aerial photograph (1972); 1 photocopy of fire photograph (c. 1935); 5 ext. photos (1974).

Buckeye Manufacturing Company (HAER IN-35), W. side Columbia Ave., between 18th and 19th Sts. Built 1904; partially destroyed 1969. Produced Lambert automobile 1905–07. 1 sheet (1972, showing 1910 plan, present elevations); 4 ext. photos (1974).

Rider-Lewis Motor Car Company (HAER IN-38), N. side W. 2nd St., at Sycamore St. Brick, two-story office building; one-story factory; king-post trussing. Built 1909; manufactured Rider-Lewis automobile 1909–10. 1 sheet (1972, plan, section, elevations); 12 ext. photos (1974), 1 int. photo (1974).

Speed Changing Pulley Company (DeTamble Motors Company) (HAER IN-36), N. side 32nd St., E. of E. Lynn St. Brick, two-story office building; one-story factory. Manufactured DeTamble automobile 1909–12. 1 sheet (1972, plan, elevations); 1 photocopy of ext. photograph (c. 1964); 7 ext. photos (1974), 2 int. photos (1974).

Aurora Vicinity   **Dearborn (15) and Ohio (58) Counties**

Laughery Creek Bridge (HAER IN-16), spanning Laughery Creek, just W. of State Rt. 56, 2.5 mi SE. of Aurora. Iron, triple-intersection Pratt through-truss, diagonal members each cross three panels. Built 1878 by Wrought Iron Bridge Co., Canton, Ohio; Henry Fitch, engineer. Oldest known surviving metal truss bridge in Indiana. 15 ext. photos (1974). NR

Brownsville   **Union County (81)**

Brownsville Covered Bridge (Wagon Bridge) (HAER IN-27), spanning E. Fork of Whitewater River, on Main St. Frame, Long truss. Built 1837–40; dismantled 1974. Only example of a Long truss bridge in Indiana.

Cannelton   **Perry County (62)**

Cannelton Cotton Mills (Indiana Cotton Mills) (HAER IN-1), 250' SW. of Fourth St., between Adams and Washington Sts. Stone, three stories on a raised basement with paired six-story towers at entrance, Lombard Romanesque style. Built between 1847 and 1849; Thomas A. Tefft, architect. Mill began manufacturing cotton goods in 1850 and operated continuously until 1954. 8 sheets (1973–74, including site plan, plans, elevation); 1 photocopy of architect's original drawing (c. 1848); 1 photocopy of aerial photograph (n.d.); 1 photocopy of ext. photograph (n.d.); 21 ext. photos (1974), 12 int. photos (1974). NR

Cannelton Cotton Mills, Superintendent's House (HAER IN-1A), N. corner Front and Washington Sts. Built 1850–51; part of Cannelton Cotton Mill complex; demolished after 1974. 3 ext. photos (1974). NR (Cannelton Cotton Mills)

Indiana Cotton Mills, Workers' Housing (A) (HAER IN-1B), NE. side Fourth St., between Washington and Taylor Sts. Frame row houses constructed 1855 for mill workers; demolished after 1974. 4 ext. photos (1974).

Indiana Cotton Mills, Workers' Housing (B) (HAER IN-1C), SW. side Fifth St., between Washington and Taylor Sts. Built 1855; similar to Fourth St. housing; demolished after 1974. Photos (1974).

Clay City   **Clay County (11)**

Eel River Bridge (Feederdam Bridge) (HAER IN-21), spanning Eel River, just W. of State Rt. 59, 4 mi. N. of Clay City. Iron, Pratt (Whipple) through-truss. Built 1894 by C. F. Hunt Co., Indianapolis. 13 ext. photos (1974).

Columbus   **Bartholomew County (3)**

Cerealine Manufacturing Company, Mill A (HAER IN-34), between Jackson and Brown Sts., opposite 7th St. Brick on stone foundation, four stories. Built c. 1880. Produced cold breakfast cereal made from corn. 2 sheets (1972, site plan, plans, sections, elevations); 4 ext. photos (1974), 1 int. photo (1974).

Reeves Pulley Company (HAER IN-15), S. side 7th St., at Wilson St. Built c. 1890; original structure absorbed by later additions and alterations. Produced variable speed transmission using patented conical pulleys that is still manufactured virtually unchanged. 1 sheet (1972, plan, sections, elevations), 1 photocopy of artist's rendering (c. 1910); 1 ext. photo (1974), 12 int. photos (1974).

Connersville   **Fayette County (21)**

Ansted-Higgins Spring Company (Ansted Spring and Axle Company) (HAER IN-9), between Mount and 16th Sts., E. of Columbia Ave. Brick, one story with moniter roof. Built 1891. First factory constructed in Connersville Industrial Park; was a supplier to McFarlan Carriage Co. 2 photocopies of artist's rendering (1906).

Central Manufacturing Company (HAER IN-10), N. side 18th St., W. of Western Ave. Built 1906, 1917; now absorbed by modern additions and alterations. Manufactured automobile bodies in wood and later in metal. 1 photocopy of artist's rendering (1906); 1 photocopy of ext. photograph (1928); 1 photocopy of wooden body assembly line (c. 1906).

Connersville Blower Company (HAER IN-13), W. side Columbia Ave., N. of Mount St. Brick, one story with moniter roof. Built 1893; exterior relatively unaltered. Company was primary competitor of P. H. and F. M. Roots Co. (HAER IN-3). 1 photocopy of artist's rendering (1906); 1 photocopy of ext. photograph (1911).

Connersville Furniture Company (HAER IN-12), E. side Illinois Ave., N. of Mount St. Brick, six stories. Built 1887; partially demolished c. 1962. Operated until 1927. 1 photocopy of artist's rendering (1906); 2 photocopies of demolition photographs (c. 1962).

Connersville Industrial Park (HAER IN-7), between 11th and 21st Sts., W. of Western Ave. Established 1886 by John B. McFarlan on farmland at edge of

Connersville. McFarlan built his factory at S. edge of park and persuaded his suppliers to build factories nearby. 1 sheet (1972, site plan); 1 photocopy of aerial photograph (1945).

Lexington Motor Company (Auburn Automobile Company) (HAER IN-11), N. side 18th St., opposite Columbia Ave. Brick, two stories, gable roof. Built 1910+. Important part of Connersville auto industry until 1930s. The classic Cord manufactured here. 4 sheets (1972, plans, elevations); 5 photocopies of ext. photographs (1920, 1928, 1929, 1931, 1936); 13 photocopies of assembly line, storage, and shipping (1934); 6 ext. photos (1974).

McFarlan Carriage Company (McFarlan Motor Car Company) (HAER IN-8), S. side Mount St., opposite Columbia Ave. Built 1886; demolished 1938–39. 1 photocopy of ext. photograph (1911).

Munk and Roberts Furniture Company (Rex Manufacturing Company) (HAER IN-14), E. side Western Ave., N. of 12th St. Built 1878; demolished 1973. Furniture, then carriages, and later auto tops and enclosures were manufactured here. 3 sheets (1972, plans, sections, elevations); 1 photocopy of artist's rendering (1906).

P. H. and F. M. Roots Company (HAER IN-3), E. side Eastern Ave. opposite 1st St. Brick; complex of factory buildings, the first constructed in 1864. Manufactured positive displacement rotary blowers. 5 sheets (1973, site plan, plan, sections, elevations); 3 photocopies of rendered map of Connersville (1856, 1875, 1888); 3 photocopies of artists' renderings (c. 1885?, 1907, 1926); 2 photocopies of int. photographs (1880, 1890?); 4 photocopies of Roots blowers (1868, 2 — 1880, 1906); photos (1974).

Crawfordsville   Montgomery County (54)

Montgomery County Jail (Old Jail Museum) (HAER IN-17), SW. corner Washington and Spring Sts. Brick, sheriff's residence with attached one-and-a-half-story jail, a cylinder iron-cage structure rotated on central axis with cells arranged on two levels. Built 1882. Oldest surviving example of unique midwestern jail type. 7 ext. photos (1974), 15 int. photos (1974).

Crawfordsville Vicinity   Montgomery County (54)

Yount Woolen Mill (HAER IN-18), W. bank Sugar Creek, 1000' S. of State Rt. 32, 4 mi. W. of Crawfordsville. Brick, two-and-a-half stories. Built 1864. Only surviving building of a small complex operated by Daniel Yount. 6 ext. photos (1974).

Cutler Vicinity (Adams Mill)   Carroll County (8)

Adams Mill Covered Bridge (HAER IN-29), spanning Wildcat Creek, on Rd. 50 E., 0.8 mi. NE. of Cutler. Frame, approx. 158', Howe trusses with added arches. Built 1872 by Wheelock Bridge Co. 5 sheets (1974, site plan, plan, sections, elevations, details).

Gosport — Owen (60) and Monroe (53) Counties

Gosport Covered Bridge (HAER IN-39), spanning White River, 500' E. of E. end South St. Frame, originally approx. 524' long, three spans, Smith trusses, one span replaced c. 1890 by double-intersection Pratt (Whipple) through-truss. Built 1870 by Smith Bridge Co.; demolished c. 1949; bridge piers remain. 1 photocopy of photograph (1913).

New Albany and Salem (Monon) Railroad, Gosport Passenger and Freight Station (HAER IN-4), E. end North St. Brick. Built c. 1854; demolished 1976. Example of early through-station; passenger tracks passed in front, freight track through entire length of structure. 3 sheets (1973, site plan, plan, elevations); 2 photocopies of ext. photographs (1896?, 1913); photos (1974).

Greensburg — Decatur County (16)

Brick Barn (HAER IN-43), State Rt. 3, S. of I-74 interchange. Brick with N. wall vertical tongue-in-groove siding, one story with loft. Unusual barn type in Midwest. 4 ext. photos (1974).

Indianapolis — Marion County (49)

Market House (Indianapolis City Market) (HAER IN-6), 222 E. Market St., N. side Market, between Delaware and Alabama Sts. Iron frame and brick. Built 1886; D. A. Bohlen, architect. Restored 1974; James Associates, architects. Surviving example of 19th C. market; notable for elegant iron columns and roof trusses fabricated by Hetherington and Berner. 6 sheets (1972, site plan, plan, sections, elevations, structural details); 5 ext. photos (1974), 9 int. photos (1974). HABS (1974) NR

Kokomo — Howard County (34)

Vermont Covered Bridge (HAER IN-30), spanning Kokomo Creek, W. end Deffenbaugh St., in Highland Park. Frame, approx. 117', single span, Smith trusses. Built c. 1874; moved 1958 from town of Vermont, Howard Co. 5 sheets (1971, site plan, plan, sections, elevations, structural details).

Lafayette — Tippecanoe County (79)

Lafayette Street Railway Powerhouse (HAER IN-41), 2 South St. Brick. Built 1892, 1896, 1907; 1892 and 1896 portions demolished 1979. One of first electric street railways in U.S.; used powerhouse to generate current to power horsecars equipped with electric motors. 3 photocopies of plans (c. 1894); 6 photocopies of int. photographs (c. 1894, c. 1911); photos (1978, 1979).

Liberty Vicinity (Dunlapsville)   Union County (81)

Dunlapsville Covered Bridge (HAER IN-31), spanning E. Fork of Whitewater River, on Roseburg Rd., 4.5 mi. SW. of Liberty. Frame, approx. 329', two spans, Burr arch trusses. Built 1870; Archibald M. Kennedy, builder; burned 1971. 6 sheets (1971, site plan, plan, sections, elevations, structural details).

Madison   Jefferson County (39)

Madison and Indianapolis Railroad, Madison Incline (Madison Cut) (HAER IN-19), starting N. of Crooked Creek, 750' W. of State Rt. 7. Built 1841. From near Crooked Creek the incline climbed 7000' at a 5.9% grade to join main line of Indiana's first railroad. 2 ext. photos (1974). NR (Madison Historic District)

Schroeder, Ben, Saddle Tree Company (HAER IN-26), 106 Milton St., N. side Milton St., 150' W. of Jefferson St. Brick. Built c. 1876. A rare, family-operated factory with original machinery operated until mid-1970s. 3 sheets (1975, site plan, plan, sections, elevation); photos (1974). NR (Madison Historic District)

Matthews   Grant County (27)

Cumberland Covered Bridge (HAER IN-32), spanning Mississinewa River, on County Rd. 990E. Frame, approx. 175', single span, Howe trusses. Built 1879 by Smith Bridge Co. 6 sheets (1970, site plan, plans, sections, elevations, structural details). NR

Montezuma Vicinity   Parke County (61)

Leatherwood Station Covered Bridge (HAER IN-40), spanning Leatherwood Creek, 3.8 mi. NE. of Montezuma. Frame, approx. 100', single span, Burr arch trusses. Built 1899; Joseph Albert Britton, builder; moved 1980–81 to Billie Creek Village, Parke Co. Photos (1979).

Paoli   **Orange County (59)**

Gospel Street Bridge (HAER IN-24), spanning Lick Creek, on S. Gospel St. Iron, single span, Pratt through-truss. Built 1890; Cleveland Bridge and Iron Co., Cleveland, Ohio. 11 ext. photos (1974).

Richmond   **Wayne County (89)**

Starr Piano Factory and Richmond Gas Company Building (HAER IN-42), adjacent to Whitewater River, between S. "G" St. and Main St. Bridges. Richmond Gas Co. building built 1854; Charles Collier, builder. Starr Piano Factory built 1872 on. Part of early industrial area using Whitewater River as source of power. Photos (1979).

Rochester Vicinity   **Fulton County (25)**

Tippecanoe River Bridge (HAER IN-25), spanning Tippecanoe River, just N. of State Rt. 25, 5 mi. NE. of Rochester. Iron, modified Pratt through-truss. Built 1890; demolished 1974. 16 ext. photos (1974).

Vera Cruz   **Wells County (90)**

Wabash River Bridge (HAER IN-22), spanning Wabash River, on State Rt. 316. Iron, double-intersection Pratt (Whipple) through-truss. Built 1887 by Indiana Bridge Co., Muncie, Indiana. 22 ext. photos (1974).

Vernon   **Jennings County (40)**

Madison and Indianapolis Railroad, Vernon Overpass (HAER IN-20), crossing Pike St., at Gains St. Stone, single span, masonry barrel arch. Part of oldest segment of Indiana's first railroad; earliest known railroad bridge in Indiana. 5 ext. photos (1974). NR (Vernon Historic District)

Versailles Vicinity   **Ripley County (69)**

Busching Covered Bridge (HAER IN-33), spanning Laughery Creek, on Covered Bridge Rd., 0.7 mi. E. of Versailles, at Versailles State Park. Frame, approx. 184', single span, Howe trusses. Built 1885; Thomas A. Hardman, builder. 3 sheets (1973, site plan, plan, sections, elevations, structural details).

Washington   **Daviess County (14)**

Ohio and Mississippi (later Baltimore and Ohio) Railroad, Washington Repair Shops
(HAER IN-5), W. end Van Trees St., at 17th St. Brick. Built 1889. Complex
served as major repair center and B & O line between Cincinnati and St.
Louis. 6 sheets (1973, site plan, plan, sections, elevations, section perspective,
roof truss details); 1 photocopy of site plan (1921); 1 photocopy of aerial
photograph (c. 1926); 28 ext. photos (1974), 4 int. photos (1974).

West Baden Springs   **Orange County (59)**

West Baden Springs Hotel (Northwood Institute) (HAER IN-2), W. side State
Rt. 56. Steel-trussed dome, 195′ diameter, covered circular atrium surrounded by guest rooms, six stories. 8 sheets (1973, 1974, site plan, plans,
sections, elevations, truss details); 19 ext. photos (1974), 32 int. photos
(1974). HABSI NR

Appendix C: HABS, HABSI, HAER Projects in Indiana Counties, by Region

Northern Region

Adams County (1)
Geneva Vicinity
    HABS Ceylon Covered Bridge

Allen County (2)
Fort Wayne
    HABS Ewing, William G., House (demolished)
    HABS Swinney, Col. Thomas W., House
Fort Wayne Vicinity
    HABS Aboite Township District School No. 5
    HABS Pleasant Township School

Carroll County (8)
Cutler Vicinity (Adams Mill)
    HAER Adams Mill Covered Bridge

Fulton County (25)
Rochester
    HABSI Fulton County Courthouse
Rochester Vicinity
    HAER Tippecanoe River Bridge (demolished)

Grant County (27)
Matthews
    HAER Cumberland Covered Bridge

Howard County (34)
Kokomo
    HAER Vermont Covered Bridge

Huntington County (35)
Huntington
    HABS House of Chief Richardville

Kosciusko County (43)
Warsaw
    HABSI Kosciusko County Courthouse

LaGrange County (44)
LaGrange
    HABSI LaGrange County Courthouse
Mongo
    HABS O'Ferrell, John, Store

Lake County (45)
Crown Point
    HABSI Lake County Courthouse
Hobart Vicinity
    HABSI Wolf, Josephus, House

La Porte County (46)
La Porte
    HABSI La Porte County Courthouse
Michigan City
    HABS Michigan City Lighthouse
New Carlisle Vicinity
    HABS Brown-Augustine House (burned)
Pinola Vicinity
    HABS/HABSI Ames-Paton House

Marshall County (50)
Plymouth
    HABSI Marshall County Courthouse

Porter County (64)
Chesterton Vicinity
    HABSI Baileytown School, District No. 5 (demolished)
Porter Vicinity
    HABS Augsburg Swensk Skola
    HABS/HABSI Bailly, Joseph, Homestead

St. Joseph County (71)
Mishawaka
    HABS 100 Block of North Main Street (demolished)
    HABS 100 Block of North Main Street, Mishawaka Trust and Savings Co. (demolished)
    HABS 100 Block of North Main Street, 107–109 N. Main Street (demolished)
    HABS 100 Block of North Main Street, Kamm Building (demolished)
    HABS 100 Block of North Main Street, 113 N. Main Street (demolished)
    HABS 100 Block of North Main Street, 115 N. Main Street (demolished)
    HABS 100 Block of North Main Street, 117–119 N. Main Street (demolished)
    HABS 100 Block of North Main Street, 121–125 N. Main Street (demolished)
    HABS 100 Block of North Main Street, 111 W. First Street (demolished)
South Bend
    HABS/HABSI Second St. Joseph County Courthouse

Wabash County (85)
North Manchester
    HABS North Manchester Public Library

Warrick County (87)
Newburgh
    HABSI Bethell, Thomas F., House
    HABS/HABSI Roberts, Gaines Hardy, House

Wells County (90)
Bluffton
    HABSI Wells County Courthouse
Vera Cruz
    HAER Wabash River Bridge

Central Region

Clay County (11)
Clay City
    HAER Eel River Bridge (Feederdam Bridge)

Decatur County (16)
Greensburg
    HAER Brick Barn
    HABSI Decatur County Courthouse

Delaware County (18)
Muncie
    HABS Administration Building, Ball State University
Muncie Vicinity
    HABS Garner, Job, House

Fayette County (21)
Connersville
    HAER Ansted-Higgins Spring Company
    HABS Canal House
    HAER Central Manufacturing Company (partially demolished)
    HAER Connersville Blower Company
    HAER Connersville Furniture Company
    HAER Connersville Industrial Park
    HAER Lexington Motor Company
    HAER McFarlan Carriage Company (demolished)
    HAER Munk and Roberts Furniture Company (demolished)
    HAER P. H. and F. M. Roots Company
    HABSI Smith, Oliver H., House
Connersville Vicinity
    HABS/HABSI Gray House
Waterloo Vicinity
    HABS Ranck Round Barn

Franklin County (24)
Brookville Vicinity
    HABSI Little Cedar Grove Baptist Church

139

Fairfield Vicinity
    HABS Logan, William, Cabin (dismantled; moved to Treaty Line Museum, Dunlapsville, Union Co. (81))
Metamora
    HABS Whitewater Canal Aqueduct

Hamilton County (29)
Noblesville
    HABSI Stone, Judge Earl S., House
Noblesville Vicinity
    HABS Conner Prairie Pioneer Settlement
    HABS/HABSI Conner Prairie Pioneer Settlement, William Conner House
    HABS Conner Prairie Pioneer Settlement, Loom House
    HABS Conner Prairie Pioneer Settlement, Still House
    HABS Conner Prairie Pioneer Settlement, Trading Post (Nichols Homestead)
    HABS Conner Prairie Pioneer Settlement, Doan House

Henry County (33)
New Castle
    HABSI Henry County Courthouse

Madison County (48)
Anderson
    HAER Anderson Carriage Manufacturing Company (burned)
    HAER Buckeye Manufacturing Company (partially demolished)
    HAER Rider-Lewis Motor Car Company
    HAER Speed Changing Pulley Company
Pendleton Vicinity
    HABS Fussell, Samuel, Log House

Marion County (49)
Indianapolis
    HABS/HABSI Allison, James A., House
    HABSI Bals-Wocher House
    HABS/HABSI Bates-Hendricks House
    HABSI Butler, David, House
    HABS/HABSI Christ (Episcopal) Church
    HABS Cole Motor Car Company Factory
    HABS Crown Hill Cemetery, Chapel and Vault
    HABS Crown Hill Cemetery, Gateway
    HABS Crown Hill Cemetery, Waiting Station
    HABS Das Deutsche Haus
    HABS Despa House
    HABS Duesenberg Automobile Company Factory
    HABS Elliott's Block
    HABSI Fletcher House (demolished)
    HABS/HABSI Harrison, Benjamin, House
    HABS Holler, George and Netty, House
    HABS/HABSI Indiana Central State Hospital, Pathological Department Building
    HABS Indiana National Bank (demolished)

140

HABS Indiana Theater
HABSI Julian, George W., House
HABS Macy, David, House (demolished)
HABS Maennerchor Building (demolished)
HABS/HAER Market House
HABS/HABSI Morris-Butler House
HABS/HABSI Nickum, John R., House
HABSI Ohmer-Benton House
HABSI Old Federal Building
HABS Prosser House
HABSI Second Presbyterian Church (demolished)
HABS Soldiers and Sailors Monument
HABS Sommers, Charles B., House
HABS Star Service Shop (demolished)
HABS Staub, Joseph W., House
HABS Union Station
HABS U.S. Arsenal, Arsenal Building
HABS Vinton-Pierce House (demolished)
HABS Webber House
HABS West, John, House
HABS Woodruff Place

Montgomery County (54)
Alamo Vicinity
HAER Deer Mill Covered Bridge
Crawfordsville
HABSI Lane, Henry S., House
HAER Montgomery County Jail
Crawfordsville Vicinity
HAER Yount Woolen Mill

Owen County (60)
Gosport
HAER Gosport Covered Bridge (demolished)
HAER New Albany and Salem (Monon) Railroad, Gosport Passenger
and Freight Station (demolished)

Parke County (61)
Montezuma Vicinity
HAER Leatherwood Station Covered Bridge (moved to Billy Creek Village, Parke County)
Turkey Run State Park
HABS Narrows Covered Bridge

Randolph County (68)
Ridgeville
HABS Ridgeville Switching Station (demolished)

Rush County (70)
Mays Vicinity
HABSI Hall, William, House
Rushville
HABS Melodeon Hall

141

Rushville Vicinity
HABS Kennedy Covered Bridge (demolished)

Shelby County (73)
Finley Vicinity
HABSI Copple, Daniel, House

Tippecanoe County (79)
Lafayette
HABSI Ball, James, Homestead
HABSI Fowler, Moses, House
HAER Lafayette Street Railway Powerhouse (partially demolished)
HABSI Tippecanoe County Courthouse

Union County (81)
Brownsville
HAER Brownsville Covered Bridge (dismantled)
Liberty
HABSI Nixson, John S., House
Liberty Vicinity (Dunlapsville)
HAER Dunlapsville Covered Bridge (burned)

Vigo County (84)
Terre Haute
HABSI Dewees, Maj. George W., House
HABSI Houriet, Lucien, House

Wayne County (89)
Cambridge City
HABS Conklin House
Centerville
HABS Julian, Judge Jacob, House
HABS Lantz House
HABS Mansion House
HABS Wayne County Warden's House and Jail
Fountain City
HABS/HABSI Coffin, Levi, House
Milton Vicinity
HABS Daniels House
HABS Kinsey, Isaac, House and Farm
Mount Auburn
HABS/HABSI Huddleston House
Pennville
HABS Coffee Pot Restaurant
Richmond
HABS Adams, Richard, House
HABS Bethel A. M. E. Church
HABS City Market (demolished)
HABS Earlham College Observatory
HABS Harrison, Thomas, House (demolished)
HABS Hicksite Friends Meeting House
HABS Raukoph House
HABS Scott, Andrew F., House
HABS Starr Historic District Study

HAER Starr Piano Factory and Richmond Gas Company Building
HABS Wayne County Courthouse
HABS Working-Class Houses

Southern Region

Bartholomew County (3)
Columbus
    HABS Zaharako's Confectionary
    HAER Cerealine Manufacturing Company, Mill A
    HAER Reeves Pulley Company

Clark County (10)
Jeffersonville
    HABS Grisamore House

Crawford County (13)
Alton Vicinity
    HAER Mill Creek Bridge

Daviess County (14)
Washington
    HAER Ohio and Mississippi (later Baltimore and Ohio) Railroad, Washington Repair Shops

Dearborn County (15)
Aurora
    HABSI "Hillforest"
Lawrenceburg
    HABSI Dearborn County Courthouse
    HABSI Vance-Tousey House

Dearborn (15) and Ohio (58) Counties
Aurora Vicinity
    HAER Laughery Creek Bridge

Floyd County (22)
New Albany
    HABS Smith, Isaac, House

Harrison County (31)
Corydon
    HABS Old State Capitol

Jefferson County (39)
Hanover
    HABSI Crowe, John Finley, House
    HABSI Hanover College YMCA Building
Madison
    HABS Area Study
    HABS Bruning Carriage House
    HABS Christ Episcopal Church
    HABS Colby-Jeffery House
    HABS Costigan, Francis, House

HABS Devenish-Haigh House
HABS Eagle Cotton Mill
HABS East Main Street Block
HABS East Main Street Row Houses
HABS Eckert, John, House
HABS Fair Play Fire Company No. 1
HABS First Baptist Church
HABS First Presbyterian Church
HABS Foster Building
HABS Frevert-Schnaitter House
HABS Hutchings, Dr. William D., Office
HABS Jefferson County Jail and Sheriff's House
HABS/HABSI Lanier, James F. D., House
HAER Madison and Indianapolis Railroad, Madison Incline
HABS McNaughton House
HABS Miller Wagon Manufacturing Shop
HABS Mulberry Street Block
HABS Pittsburgh, Cincinnati, Chicago and St. Louis Railway Company
    Station
HABS Robinson-Schofield House
HABS Saint Michael's Catholic Church
HABS Saint Michael's Rectory
HAER Schroeder, Ben, Saddle Tree Company
HABS Second Presbyterian Church
HABS/HABSI Shrewsbury, Charles L., House
HABS Shuh, Jacob, House
HABS Sullivan, Jeremiah, House
HABS Talbott, Richard, House
HABS Walnut Street Fire Company No. 4
HABS Washington Fire Company No. 2
HABS West Main Street Block
Madison Vicinity
HABS Bachman House

Jennings County (40)
Vernon
HABSI Jennings County Courthouse
HAER Madison and Indianapolis Railroad, Vernon Overpass

Knox County (42)
Vincennes
HABS Brouillet, Michael, House
HABS/HABSI College of Vincennes, Saint Rose Chapel
HABSI Ellis, Judge Abner T., Mansion
HABS/HABSI "Grouseland"
HABSI Knox County Courthouse
HABS Saint Francis Xavier Cathedral
HABS/HABSI Saint Francis Xavier, Library
HABS Saint Francis Xavier, Priests' House
HABSI State Bank of Indiana
HABSI Territory Hall

Lawrence County (47)
Mitchell
    HABS Riley School (demolished)

Monroe County (53)
Bloomington
    HABS Wylie, Andrew, House
    HABSI Woodburn-Wells House
Bloomington Vicinity
    HABSI Stout, Daniel, House

Ohio (58) *and Dearborn* (15) *Counties*
Aurora Vicinity
    HAER Laughery Creek Bridge

Orange County (59)
Paoli
    HABS/HABSI Orange County Courthouse
    HAER Gospel Street Bridge
West Baden Springs
    HABSI/HAER West Baden Springs Hotel

Perry County (62)
Cannelton
    HAER Cannelton Cotton Mills (Indiana Cotton Mills)
    HAER Cannelton Cotton Mills, Superintendent's House (demolished)
    HAER Indiana Cotton Mills, Workers' Housing (A) (demolished)
    HAER Indiana Cotton Mills, Workers' Housing (B) (demolished)
Dexter Vicinity
    HABSI Springer, Joseph, House (ruins)

Posey County (65)
New Harmony
    HABSI Log House
    HABS Owen, David Dale, House
    HABS Rapp-Maclure-Owen House
    HABS Rappite Community House No. 2
    HABS Rappite Community House No. 2 Annex
    HABS Rappite Community House No. 3 (demolished)
    HABS Rappite Community House No. 4
    HABS Rappite Granary
    HABSI Rappite House (David Lenz House)
    HABS Rappite House (Poet's House)
    HABS Rappite House (Rawlings House)
    HABS Rappite House (Salomon Wolf House)
    HABS Schnee House (demolished)
    HABS Vondegrift House (1830 Owen House)

Ripley County (69)
Morris Vicinity
    HABS Nobbe, Marie K., House
Versailles Vicinity
    HAER Busching Covered Bridge

Switzerland County (78)

Vevay

 HABS/HABSI Dufour, John Francis, House (demolished)

 HABS Ruter Chapel

 HABS/HABSI Schenck, Ulysses P., House

 HABSI Switzerland County Courthouse

 HABS Switzerland Couty Courthouse Privy

Vevay Vicinity

 HABSI Dufour, John David, House (burned)

 HABSI Wright, John W., House

Vanderburgh County (82)

Evansville

 HABS Carpenter, Willard, House

 HABSI Heilman, William, House

 HABSI Viele, Charles, House

 HABSI Willard Library

Washington County (88)

Salem

 HABS Old Salem School (John Hay Birthplace)

Appendix D: Maps Showing Indiana Counties, by Region

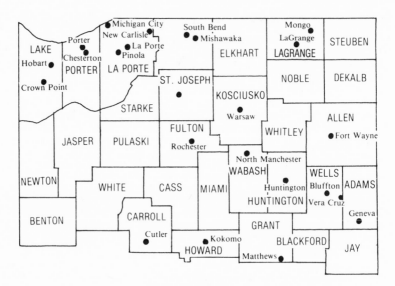

Northern Region

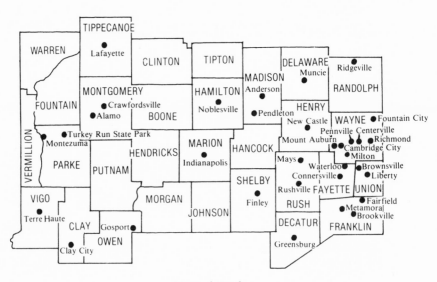

Central Region

Southern Region

Index

Page numbers in bold type indicate illustrations.